I Will Never Leave You

Memoirs of Surviving Grief through Spirit Communication

Rev. Dee Massengale, DD, M.Ed, MA

AuthorHouse™
1663 Liberty Drive
Bloomington, IN 47403
www.authorhouse.com
Phone: 1-800-839-8640

All names of co-workers and patients have been changed.

© 2012 Rev. Dee Massengale, DD, M.Ed, MA. All rights reserved.

No part of this book may be reproduced, stored in a retrieval system, or transmitted by any means without the written permission of the author.

Published by AuthorHouse 10/22/2012

ISBN: 978-1-4772-7408-8 (e)
ISBN: 978-1-4772-7409-5 (hc)
ISBN: 978-1-4772-7410-1 (sc)

Library of Congress Control Number: 2012917765

Front cover art by Martha Rampley
Author Headshot by Terrell Torrence'

This book is printed on acid-free paper.

Because of the dynamic nature of the Internet, any web addresses or links contained in this book may have changed since publication and may no longer be valid. The views expressed in this work are solely those of the author and do not necessarily reflect the views of the publisher, and the publisher hereby disclaims any responsibility for them.

www.griefresolution.com

I dedicate this book to Marial Monyjok Yak, the soft spirit who, in life, taught me how to be a kinder, more patient person, who, in death, taught me to find the peace that lies within. I have learned that the energy of love can never be dissolved. The strength that I have gained from signs and messages from the other side has allowed me to survive the subsequent loss of my mother, godfather, cousin, Marial's mother, and my dog (all of whom died within eighteen months) with a spiritual grace that I would never have thought possible. I am never alone, because God and my loved ones go with me wherever I go. This I *just know.*

Table of Contents

My story. 1
Life after death starts to present its case 15
My second trip to Africa. 31
Paranormal photography. 63
Healing from the other side 87
Grief 123

Preface

To fully appreciate the powerful impact Marial Monyjok Yak, also known as Gabriel Konga Bol, has had on the lives of everyone who knew him, it is important for you to really understand who he was. I know of no better way than to share the autobiography he wrote when applying to Emory University. This is his story, unedited, in his words.

I am a refugee survivor of the civil war in Sudan. The media refers to me and thousands like me as the "Lost Boys of Sudan." For the last four years, I have had the privilege to live in America. It has, however, been a daily ordeal waging countless, unforgettable reflections of the longest crusade in modern-day history. I have been overwhelmed with great joy at my new life in America and all its opportunities, but the most intended fight for me has been to stop thinking about surviving the prison of war and life in a refugee camp for almost a decade. The death of and separation from of my parents, sisters, brothers, uncles, cousins, and countless other relatives are a never-ending burden on my soul.

In Southern Sudan, Black Christians and the Northern Arab Muslims have been immersed in civil war for over twenty-five years. The mass executions of southern Sudanese were ongoing dramatic events, but the most unforgettable day was the destruction of my town. Burning of villages that escalated to the rape and murder of all the women and children. Rebels are known as the SPLA, or the Sudan People's Liberation Army; they tried to protect our freedom from Islamic law but could not defend the innocents from torture and dehumanization. To survive I had to eat unthinkable things and had only a tree to sleep under, all without the love and care of my mother.

Rev. Dee Massengale, DD, M.Ed, MA

I have not been interested in sharing my long and sad stories of surviving, even though classmates and American friends constantly ask me about them. I blench and prefer to keep these unimaginable events and memories for my grave. It may ruin someone's life to know the details. My only driving force on a daily basis is to pretend these things never happened. You see, my childhood was stolen, and all I have is a desire for an education. We are called Lost Boys because we are lost from our parents. *Education is my mother and father* is the slogan we have come to live by.

It is this hunger that brought the United Nations to deliver some of us to America in 2001. I learned to write my ABCs in the dirt. Once in the refugee camp, we were offered a school but not a school as you know it. There was a simple tent to shelter us from the desert sun. There were no books or labs. There was no breakfast or lunch, but there was the most precious of resources: a teacher. We studied and learned all we could.

But why did I end up in America and my brother did not? Why did I survive when most of my family did not? What is the purpose of living? These questions are significant and annoying to my daily life. I have an extended determination to find the answers. It is this inspiration that drives me to apply to a highest institution such as Emory University. My aspiration is to become a doctor or health care provider and support humanity in every way I possibly can. I survived for a reason, and that reason must be to make a difference in this world. I must have a good education to achieve that goal and to direct me toward convalescing from my untreatable illness, which is my sad background and experiences.

Thank you for listening to my story.

In grieving the loss of a close loved one, a firm belief in the afterlife that the soul is immortal and the energy of that soul lives on, greatly enhances the coping mechanisms of the individual physically, emotionally, and psychosocially. This is based on personal experiences such as seeing, hearing, and smelling the loved one but may also include paranormal experiences such as picking up a ringing phone to discover only silence; witnessing the TV or radio turn on by itself; seeing clocks tick in reverse time, just to name a few. Note there is a profound difference in experiencing an "inexplicable" experience that leads a person to an ineffable sense of knowing it is the presence of the deceased versus the bereaved person who says his loved one is "in a better place" simply because that is what he was taught in a house of worship. My thesis is that the feeling of *just knowing* that the energy of our loved one is still with us can have a profound effect on our ability to cope, rationalize, and simply deal with such a great void in our life, and there is no more effective way to come to this conclusion than through personal experience.

"If anything were ever to happen to you, I would just die. Please do not drive fast and wear your seat belt!" Those words were to become prophetic, as you will see, in my story.

My story

The unexplainable bonds of love began in 2001. As a volunteer for the International Rescue Committee, I was actively involved in helping to resettle and orient a group of young refugee men called the Lost Boys of Sudan. These remarkable refugees were called Lost Boys because they had been separated from their parents as very young children due to a long and violent civil war in Southern Sudan. They had walked a thousand miles from one refugee camp to another trying to escape death—not only from bullets but also animal attacks, dehydration, and starvation.

After learning the details of their painful past, I was struck by their impeccable manners. They always greeted me with a handshake, a big smile, and eye contact, and soon, they even referred to me as Momma Dee, an indication they recognized, and appreciated the fact that I was there to assist them along their incredible journey of adapting to modern life in America. At age forty-five with no children of my own, it was a match made in heaven.

One beautiful May afternoon, I had taken clothes to an apartment of newcomers that were not home. I laid out a variety of shirts, pants, and socks on each bed. As I was leaving, a very tall, super skinny man walked through the door. In a shy manner, he tilted his head and quietly said, "Hello, my name is Gabriel." He reached his hand out for mine. I simply responded, "Oh, like the angel." Little did I know how true that statement was to become! My life was never to be the same. For, in fact, on that glorious May day ... I did meet an angel.

As a volunteer, I was the busiest I had ever been in my life. The boys, as we called them, had so many demands. I would receive calls saying they were out of toilet paper and could I take them to the store. Never mind that I lived thirty minutes away by interstate—I would drop what I was doing and go. Of course, no refugee has a car the first year; it takes a while to buy your first two-thousand-dollar lemon when you only get paid eight dollars an hour. So I drove. I was on a crazy "prevent any more suffering mission." When I was not acting as their taxi, I was out begging for donations. They needed everything from the bare essentials to TVs and computers. This world was so new, and their needs were truly overwhelming. I did what I could and prayed for the rest.

Gabriel was different. He called every morning at 9:00 during his break at work, but it was not to ask for anything. Day after the day, the conversation went like this: "Good morning, how are you? How is your mom? How is Trevor [my husband at the time]? How is your dog?" He knew very little English, so I was satisfied with our morning chats. I really did appreciate that he took the time to acknowledge me and perhaps what I was doing for him and the rest of his "brothers." An inexplicable bond started to form. The other guys began to notice and would tease him saying things like, "Oh, you are her favorite." The question was: if this was true why? He was not the most handsome among them; he was not as outgoing and gregarious as others; his English was poor and communication was difficult. He seemed like a little bird that had fallen from his nest, broken his wing, and was trying to learn to fly. There were others who stood out as leaders and scholars. In fact, many eventually succeeded in University, wrote books, built schools, and made those of us who "knew them then" very proud. What I would not learn until a year later is that unlike the others, Gabriel had only obtained a third-grade education in the camp. It would not be until 2004, when I went to Africa to meet his brother that I would learn why.

He had been taken as a child soldier when he was ten years old. For many of the years that the other Lost Boys were studying in the camp, Gabriel was forced to live an unthinkable life. Those painful years left scars that I would not truly comprehend until after his death. This gentle soul had been to hell and back.

Maternal Instincts

One day in late July, Gabriel called to say he had fallen off his bike and hurt his knee. He sounded like a little boy who wanted his momma to fix it. Being a rehabilitation therapist, I told him to put some ice on it and that I would be there in thirty minutes. I was thinking a meniscus tear or patella subluxation. It had to be something serious or he would not have called, right? Well, as usual, I dropped what I was doing and drove to Clarkston, the small town outside Atlanta where the refugees live. I just could not bear the thought that dear sweet Gabriel was injured and suffering in any way. I knew full well they all had suffered enough to last a hundred lifetimes. When I arrived, I found Gabriel's knee had a full range of motion and no swelling or tenderness. There was no joint laxity; it was just a skinned knee and a drop of blood. Gabriel was distraught because the brakes had failed, and he was frightened as he flew downhill into a tree. What was more remarkable than his reaction to the event was mine. In my forty-six years, I was experiencing my first real maternal instincts; my boy was suffering, and I would do anything to ease his fear and pain. It was if a magnet was pulling us together. I did not recognize it at the time, as I was involved with so many of the Lost Boys' lives and dramas. It was, however, a turning point in what has proved to be a very real soul connection.

The ultimate act of maternal care proved to be my affirmative response some weeks later when he asked me to teach him to drive. Oh my goodness in my BMW! We started in a church parking lot hoping sacred ground would work in our favor. When we finally hit the streets,

Gabriel drove so slowly that I was afraid we would be run over by a box turtle. Little did I know as I begged him to go faster that speed would end his young life eight years later.

I love you

Gabriel had been in the United State for six months. We sat in my car after a driving lesion and he told me that his best friend in Boston wanted him to move up there so they could live together. He had replied, "No, I have to stay in Atlanta because I need Mom Dee to teach me how to be an American." It took everything in me not to burst out into tears. What an honor, what a responsibility! It was very clear he wanted to fit in, to truly be a part of something that he respected and cherished. I asked him what he had learned about America when he was in Africa. His response was chilling: "America is where all the food comes from." He went on to explain that bags of food would be dropped from airplanes that said USA. In their hungry minds, America was a country full of abundant food. What could be more ideal when you're starving? I was already speechless when he softly said under his breath, "I love you." What did this mean? Was there a misconception of my role? I simply could not respond, as I did not understand the context of the message. I said nothing, but was soon to discover it simply meant, "I trust you to take care of me," and so I did. It was an honor and a blessing that changed my life. About two months later, Gabriel called to say he had a severe toothache. I quickly got him to one of our fabulous volunteer providers, a peridontist we called Dr. Gail. After an extensive exam, she came to me and said that X-rays showed he could be quite a bit younger than his INS stated (which he had said all along). This was great news in terms of education, because if I could prove he was seventeen, I could get him enrolled in high school. His immigration listed his age as twenty-four, which was too old to obtain a GED through Job Corp and way to old too to start high school. Things happened quickly. Dr.

Gail wrote a letter suggesting his age was seventeen, and the next thing I knew we were at the Fulton County Courthouse in Atlanta and I was obtaining legal guardianship. An unforeseen problem was brought to light. He lived in DeKalb County and I in Fulton. I could not lie, and he could not go to school in his county with his guardian in another. Okay, I said, you will have to come and live with us. He readily agreed, but there was the issue of my husband, with whom I was not getting along very well, and my elderly mom, who frankly hated houseguests of any sort! What would they think of a permanent houseguest? I decided my mom would be a lost cause, so I opted out not to ask. She had dementia and maybe my blind faith was hoping she would not notice there was another man, an African man, living in the guest bedroom. I asked my husband if it was okay for Gabriel to move in so that he could attend high school. He cleverly responded, "Well, it is your house, and you are going to do what you want to do regardless of what I say," which was true. It was my house and he had done little to support it or me, so the decision was made! Gabriel would move in.

The daunting task was upon me to tell my mom. At eighty-four, change was just not in her vocabulary, so I decided to tell her rather than to ask, based on the saying that it is easier to get forgiveness than permission. To my shock, she was genuinely delighted. In retrospect, the only explanation of her reaction was that she felt the soul connection too!

Two days later, the guest room was filled with blue jeans, T-shirts, and really big athletic shoes. We went to North Atlanta High School, and Gabriel registered for the ninth grade. His dream of obtaining an education was finally coming true.

> Thank you for help.
> I apprericiate.
> Your help is Great.
> Wishing your lifetime
> of happiness. and wonder
> Full bless.
> Congratatation to you.
> You are Real wonderffull
> A Person.
> You safe my life.
>   Sincenly. Gabrel Bol

Gabriel hand written letter thanking me for getting him into school.

Getting on the Bus

Gabriel made the difficult decision to drop his car insurance since he would no longer be working and would not have dreamed of asking us to pay for it. His car would sit at the foot of my driveway for three years. Every morning, he walked to the end of my street to wait on the bus. Only a week had gone by when he made fun of himself in a jovial way, telling his morning tale. "All these white people are driving by looking at me and wondering what in the world is this Black boy doing standing at the street corner," he said. He was not at all offended by the stares but seriously amused. He knew he looked different in my neighborhood; he even looked different at the predominately Black high school simply due to the rich, dark color of his skin. He continued to smile and greet anyone who would make eye contact, and soon he was the neighborhood's new favorite son!

At school, he was initially treated with resistance by a lot of the African American students. They made fun of him by calling him "Jungle Bunny" and teased him about being so skinny. They even tried to pull his pants down, as they were barely hanging on. Gabriel figured out how to handle it. He didn't go to the teacher, and he didn't start a fight, which he would have won because he was about five or six inches taller than the bullies and had combat training. No, he just killed them with kindness and acceptance. It was unbelievable.

It was only a couple of weeks after the biology teacher called me in for a meeting to discuss the bullying that girls started to phone him, inviting him to church and family dinners. The boys started to embrace this strange newcomer, asking him about his past, to which he would reply, "I cannot tell you about my past because it will ruin your life." That's right; instead of looking for pity, he protected the children by keeping the details of death, torture, and starvation, separation from parents, and war from them. In reality, this is just a subtle example of the angel he was.

Starting school in the middle of the year, in the ninth grade with a refugee camp's third grade education was daunting to say the least. The ESL (English as Second Language) teacher called me about a month into the semester to report that Gabriel would probably never catch up, and at the very least it would take five years. I took the path of least resistance ... denial and never told Gabriel. Long story short, through hours upon hours of study and my tutoring in vocabulary, Gabriel went on to earn multiple awards for the most improved in English and Literature as well as Citizenship awards. He became a prime example of what sheer determination can do. By the time he graduated, he was listed in *Who's Who of American High School Students*!

Gabriel was now in his second semester of tenth grade when I felt compelled to go to Africa to meet his brother. How could the agencies that resettle refugees bring one brother and leave the other behind? Their bond was obvious, as the only money Gab ever asked me for was a five-dollar phone card to call his brother. I had been sending this brother, Deng, money for about a year so that he could be enrolled in high school. As a refugee in Kenya, education is not free. The actual ages of the Lost Boys have been incredibly ambiguous, but I think at the time I got Deng in school he was twenty-four.

By e-mail, we had planned for him to meet me at the airport when my plane landed at 11:00 p.m. The plane was on time, and I entered an empty airport, and I do mean empty, because Deng was not even there. I waited and waited then began placing calls both to him and to the bed and breakfast where I was going to be staying. To my horror, I realized that Deng's phone had been stolen. The owner of the B & B collected me, but I did not sleep a minute that night. I knew how excited Deng was to meet me and there was no way he would have missed greeting me unless something had gone terribly wrong. The next day, I learned I was right. By the grace of God I remembered his e-mail address. From my bed and breakfast, I e-mailed him my location. Within a couple of hours, he responded that he had been mugged on the way to the airport. The flowers he had bought for me and his phone had been stolen. He had slept on the street in Nairobi and began walking bewildered that morning when he ran into a classmate who gave him a few shillings to go to an Internet café where he found my message. He noted his location, and within thirty minutes my innkeepers drove me across town. As we arrived at the café, Deng was walking up an alley. He looked like Gabriel, and, with my being white, we immediately knew each other. We ran, embraced, and cried at the long-awaited union.

In the days to come, Deng and I had a lot of time to talk. Mostly I asked questions and he told me things that I had never been able to get out of Gabriel. Most shocking was that they both had been child soldiers and had suffered terribly as a result of it. When I thought the life of a Lost Boy of Sudan could not get any worse, it did! During the time they were sent away to Ethiopia for "safe haven" and some schooling, a group of soldiers approached and told the young boys that if they were to come with them they would find their parents. Of course these hungry, scared boys wanted the comfort and safety of their mothers. It was a promise that was not kept. Deng said it was the children who held watch over the village or compound, wherever they might be, all night, awaiting Arab attacks so they could fire their weapons to waken the soldiers. He described how, for years, they had slept on the cold ground with no coverings surrounded by never-ending gunfire, village raids, and the smell of death. It greatly saddened me so to think that someone I had come to love so much had suffered such horror. It literally made my commitment to protect and provide for Gabriel even stronger.

The next bombshell was to learn that Gabriel Konga Bol was not even his name. Gabriel was, in fact, Marial Monyjok Yak and was nicknamed Mike! I learned that the brothers were not brought to the States together because child soldiers were disqualified. The commission that oversees refugees was afraid those boys might not adapt well due to the trauma they had suffered. Marial, desperate to get out of what Lost Boys referred to as "Darkness Place," Kakuma Refugee Camp, assumed his cousin's identity. His cousin had been accepted as a refugee, but due to some kind of mental illness, was afraid to make the move. This explained why his INS card said he was twenty-four when he arrived; however, he had always argued that he was only eighteen or nineteen.

Marial had not shared his secret out of fear that I would disapprove of his dishonesty, but my reaction was quite to the contrary. He was a survivor; that was what he had always had to do, and this was just another act of survival.

Aside from having to digest all the shocking news, Deng and I had a great time. We went on a Safari in the Serengeti and spent a few days on the Indian Ocean in Mombasa. I did not have a lot of money to spend, so we always shared a room (two beds). Every night, Deng had nightmares that led him to scream and thrash around in his bed. I would call out to wake him. Sometimes we talked about the nightmare, but mostly he kept quiet. I had to wonder if this happened to Marial too. He slept upstairs with his door locked; I slept downstairs and had never given nightmares a thought.

When I returned to Atlanta and told Gabriel, aka Marial, all that I had learned, he was mortified. He literally shut down. It took about a week for him to relax and to get used to being called by his proper name. After a year and a half, he had his name legally changed. Shortly before graduating from high school, he told his classmates. He wanted his real name on his diploma.

His final chapter

Marial was accepted to Oxford College of Emory University, a very prestigious two-year college. He wanted nothing more than to graduate so that he could continue his studies on the main campus of Emory University in Atlanta. He lived in the library, studying day and night. He e-mailed every term paper to clean up his grammar. Remember, he had never attended the eighth grade, which is where kids study grammar. The whole situation was daunting from the beginning. Marial just did not have the educational background to compete with his Oxford classmates. I am sure he was accepted on some kind of ethnic diversity program because it sure was not based on his SAT score. It was not fair to set him up for failure, which is what I feel Oxford did. I worried about him night and day and spent countless hours on the computer and phone trying to help him with papers and projects. He was determined, he gave it his all, but he missed graduating by one point in Chemistry. I know this disappointment pierced his soul. He took up driving a cab for six months to pay off his credit card. Once again, he put 110 percent into that job, sleeping in the cab and literally staying out twenty-three hours a day. He would come home around three in the morning and take a shower. I always had some food in the microwave for him. It was an agonizing six months for both of us.

In the rare moments we had to just sit and talk, I would often bring up the subject of the afterlife. I had plenty of opinions. I was convinced that since we are all made of energy, our energy or the soul, must live on. I could go on and on about it, but all I ever got out of him was a polite stare that really said, "You are crazy." He had too much respect for me to ever tell me so, but I could read his face! I remember the day I said, "Let's make a deal. Whoever dies first will come back and let the other know that he or she is okay." He agreed, but I had to laugh, knowing that he was not taking any of it seriously. I was so wrong, as you will see.

It was now December 2008, the heart of the recession. Marial's friends were graduating from college but could not find jobs. After doing quite a bit of research online, Marial decides that becoming an air traffic controller would assure him a job, and a well-paying one at that. He had nerves of steel and the patience of Job, so I thought it might be the perfect career for him. Unfortunately this meant moving to Tulsa, Oklahoma for school. In less than a month, the car was packed, the student loan secured, and he was off. In the months to come I traveled there twice to buy him furniture and a bed, as he insisted on sleeping on the floor so I would not have to spend any money. Marial did find a part-time job in a Sprint call center to cover his basic needs, but, of course, this drastically cut into his study time.

Soon Marial would find Tulsa an unfriendly place for foreigners.

He was pulled over by the police three times: once for driving too slowly; once just to check his license; and once for simply walking across a parking lot to get into his new car. The officer asked him for his immigration card. The officer took his green card and then accused him of stealing the car. Marial insisted that the title was behind the driver's seat, but the cop refused to look. He was handcuffed and taken to jail where he sat for eleven hours until Tulsa police could verify his legal immigration status. When I learned of this, I planned to sue the police department, but his fate got in the way.

Sadly, history repeated itself. Marial missed making his grades again by a couple of points in math. When you failed a class, the school's policy was that you had to repeat the whole module over, including the classes you had passed. At two thousand dollars a module, he just could not bear it. I bought him a plane ticket and invited him to come home for his birthday and to sort out a plan. On August 28, 2009 Marial returned. My ninety-one-year-old mother and I collected him at the airport and went straight to the hospital for her pacemaker check and cardiology workup. When we arrived, I had a bizarre anxiety attack. I felt impending doom that something terrible was going to happen. I thought my mom was going to die and was paralyzed with grief. For two months prior to that day, I had experienced the occasional anxiety attack about my mother's impending death. I would wake up every night at two o'clock in the morning only to look at the clock and think to myself, "She is going to die at 2:00 a.m." I just did not know the date. My fear of losing my mom was exacerbated by the fact that I would be alone. My dad died when I was fifteen, I had no brothers or sisters, no children, no cousins in town. Even all my aunts and uncles had passed away. Over the years, I would ask Marial if he would take care of me when I was old. He always assured me that he would. He told me, "I will never leave you." It's a promise he has kept.

I asked Marial to take Mom into the hospital for me and I stayed in the car for three hours where I had a complete meltdown. Upon their return, I was feeling a bit better and we all went out for a dinner to celebrate Marial's twenty-eighth birthday. Since I had bought him a twelve thousand dollar car the month before, I did not give him a regular gift. Instead, I bought a three-dollar plastic angel with a card that said "Keep this in your pocket for protection." After dinner we came home and watched TV, had some laughs, and then he asked if he could borrow my car to go and visit friends. "Of course," I responded but I asked him to return the same night so that I could get my keys back for a dog sitting job in the morning. He told me he loved me, which we told each other daily, gave me a big hug, and ran out the door. I went to the bathroom and found the angel sitting on the sink. Not thinking much of it, I went downstairs to resume watching TV. About an hour, later I found myself upstairs walking up and down the hall chanting. In retrospect, it seemed to be a Native American language. I was wailing as if in acute grief. It was almost as if I were in a trance, because I did not question what I was doing or what was happening, but the experience was an alien one. I do not remember going to bed, but I woke at 1:30 a.m. thinking that I had not heard the car or garage door and wondered if Marial had gotten home. I went into the garage to find it empty. I phoned his best friend who, albeit the same age, was his nephew. "James, is Marial with you?" I asked.

"Yes," he replied.

I jokingly and lovingly barked, "Tell him to get his skinny Black ass home now, as I will need my keys in a few hours." I never spoke to Marial, I just went back to sleep. At six the next morning, there was still no car or sign of Marial, so I phoned James again.

"He left shortly after you called. Maybe he went to Rachel's house," James told me. So I phoned there. They had not seen him since nine o'clock the night before. Now the pit in my stomach was growing larger by the minute. He had worried the hell out of me many times before; surely he would turn up any minute with a plausible story. He did not. Instead, a detective in an unmarked black car did. I ran to the street screaming, "Is Marial okay? Did he have an accident?"

"Ma'am, come inside and sit down," he replied.

At that I yelled, "Is he dead?"

"Ma'am, come sit down." The last thing I can remember is the detective telling me he would not leave me until a friend arrived.

Marial had totaled my new car on Interstate 285. He died at 2:00 a.m. on impact of blunt force trauma to his lungs. My world was shattered; the most precious gift was taken away; the light of my life had been extinguished, and I too was surely going to die.

Life after death starts to present its case

I do not remember much of those first two days; the gut-wrenching pain of shock and grief must have killed brain cells. James did come and see me and had a friend drive me to the funeral home. James insisted on seeing Marial even though we were told he was not ready yet. After identifying the body, we went upstairs to a large table to discuss arrangements with the undertaker. The first thing he pulled out to return to me was the angel. Apparently, after I had gone back downstairs that fatal night Marial returned home to collect the angel. My heart sunk, I said, "It was supposed to protect him." Somehow I telepathically got a clear message that he was protected. He had suffered no pain and went straight to the light. The angels were there for him. This is something I just *knew*.

My friend Bennie, who got me into a psychiatrist's office four hours after receiving the news, told me later that I'd told the doctor, "My life is over." Being a licensed counselor, she knew I

This is the three-dollar angel that I gave Marial the day before the accident. Once the mortician returned it to me, I had a gold hook put on it and wore it daily for a year. Now I keep it in my purse at all times. My angel goes with me everywhere.

needed medication to get me through the next couple of weeks, and I must admit, if ever there was a time for Xanax, that was it. My blood pressure was off the charts and I could not eat, not even a bite. On the third day, I remember waking up and going to my laptop to check e-mail. My wallpaper was a picture of a waterfall, which Marial had set up for me (I knew nothing about computers). When I opened the laptop, the screen was a picture of his face. "No, this is too much," I screamed. "Too much, too soon." Somehow I inherently knew that he had done it, that he was telling me he was still with me. I had to get a neighbor to change the screen back to the waterfall because I did not know how to do it. This was the first of so many inexplicable signs from the other side. I must admit that on many levels, these signs have indeed saved my life. Nothing so strange had ever happened to me, but I have to emphasize that I just knew that somehow Marial had tampered with my computer and for my benefit.

The very same day, I was sitting in my living room with a friend and we heard birds chirping in the wall. It was a wall away from the exterior of the house, and, once again, I was overcome with a sense of knowing. It was Marial trying to communicate, trying to let me know he was there with me. In the days, months, and even years to come, these paranormal events continued. I chose to call them my miracles from heaven, as that is exactly what they were during my grief.

Chronology of my miracles from heaven

Two days before the funeral, my friend Bennie, who had taken me to the psychiatrist, had a dream. Earlier in the week she had sent me a rustic clay vase full of yellow and orange flowers. In her dream she heard Marial say, "I love the flowers," *However*, in the dream he had not spoken in English; he spoke in his native tongue of Dinka but somehow, she perhaps telepathically, understood what he was saying. On the same night, he came to me in a dream and said, "It was my time to die." It did not upset me because I knew his soul had gone through so much. He was probably tired of being shot at, tired of being racially profiled, tired of trying so hard, coming so close but not reaching his goal. I knew that Marial's conscious mind did not want to die, but somehow I understood that maybe his soul did.

The night of the wake, I was incredibly strong. I never cried, even though others were hysterical. I explained to the people there that I felt his essence of calm inside of me, and, to this day, I do believe he somehow soldiered me through that trying night. After a week of drinking myself into oblivion and crying a million tears, I was a rock. The same held true the next day at the funeral. I got up in front of a church full of Sudanese and gave a eulogy with clarity and poise. As soon as I got home, Fox 5 TV news was at my door for an interview. They ran a beautiful story full of photographs and memories honoring Marial and documenting our story. I never shed a tear in public that weekend. It was a surreal strength and I give credit to a much higher power than myself.

The trip from hell ... or to hell

Now I had the unthinkable task of driving to Tulsa, looking for his car, cleaning out his apartment, and driving back home. I was blessed with two wonderful male friends, Rick and Fred, who assisted me. For seven years (since Marial moved in), I had been terrified of the highway and interstate. I simply could not drive on either. It was a fear of speed and of having an accident. Once that fear became real with Marial's death, my fear disappeared. Logic would suggest that it should only have gotten worse, but miraculously it went away. I was no longer waking up at 2:00 a.m. either. Were these two things connected? I believe it was about the energy, the energy that bound us together. Because life and death are predetermined, I felt Marial's energy being disconnected from me months and even years before it actually was.

Once in the Tulsa airport, we had to search for his car. When I finally spotted it, I began to scream and cry uncontrollably. I could not believe that he was no longer connected with it. It was hours before the tow truck came to haul it to Honda where we had to have a key made. In the meantime, Rick drove me to Marial's apartment where I took on the daunting tasks of cleaning, collecting his clothes, and donating his furniture, which I had recently bought. It took all day, but when the task was complete and the apartment void of all his belongings, I sat down on the floor and started to cry. As I looked up, there on the floor in front of me was his social security card. Impossible! The floor had just been vacuumed moments before; nothing, and I mean nothing, had been on the floor when I finished vacuuming. To compound the mystery is the fact that Marial always kept that card in his wallet. There was no way that card could just appear on the floor unless *Marial had* put it there.

There was a knock on the door. It was his neighbor Mary from across the hall. She informed me that she had planned a surprise birthday party for Marial upon his return to Tulsa and had already bought the wine and glasses. She described how all the neighbors—young and old, Black and white—loved Marial. It came as no surprise but was comforting to hear all the same. Mary then asked if I would like a glass of wine and swiftly returned with a bottle of Turning Leaf chardonnay. I freaked out because in my completely totaled car that looked like a pancake I had found a bottle of Turning Leaf chardonnay under the drivers' seat that had not been opened and miraculously had not broken in the crash. It was another sign that his death was a turning point in my spiritual life. The message was clear early on: the deceased do send us signs; we just have to be open and receptive.

Rick and Fred finally returned from the Honda dealership, and it was time for us to head out. We planned to spend the night in Arkansas. I was a blubbering idiot, crying the whole way. When we arrived at the hotel, I pulled out my wallet to pay and there was a picture of me with beautiful flowers in the background. Marial had once told me it was his favorite picture of me, but where did it come from? I never saw it when I was cleaning out the apartment. To my knowledge, he did not even have a copy, but there it was. I was overwhelmed with the paranormal and decided it was time to unload this information on Rick for his opinion. Although he said he believed me, he just looked at me in disbelief.

After returning to Atlanta, I discovered that I could place my pendulum over any item that had been in Marial's apartment and get a positive spin, i.e. in a clockwise direction. This would happen on glass, clothes, and even a table. However, if I held the pendulum over a similar object that was not his, I got nothing. I interpreted this to mean that his energy was still within his possessions. That seemed pretty cool, so I tried talking to him with my pendulum. I first asked if he was still Black in heaven or the other side, and it swung counterclockwise, which meant no. There were so many burning questions. Did you go straight to the light? Yes. Did you suffer any pain? No. Have you seen Jesus? Marial had not been very religious. Yes. Are you happy? Yes. Wow, I thought. This other side may be a pretty good place.

And now you are a bird?

My friend Barbara thought it would be a good idea for me to have my own Web site so that I could promote my Reiki practice. God knows, I needed a diversion from my grief. I had only been back from Tulsa less than a week and had not returned to my job as a rehabilitation therapist. I chose to use the photograph of me with the beautiful flowers, which I had mysteriously found in my purse the week before in Arkansas. When the first page of the Web site was complete and my photo was uploaded, I queried, "Hey Marial, do you like the picture?" To our astonishment, we began to hear a bird chirping in the wall. As Barbara looked at me, I just smiled and said, "He approves." I felt his presence and knew he was excited about my new venture.

The following week, a regular Reiki client came for a session. She had never met Marial but did know that he had passed. This client would always see brilliant colors when I was doing Reiki on her, but on this day what happened shocked both of us. At the end of the hour she announced that Marial had spoken to her. He said, "Tell Dee I am fine; I want her to be happy; she gave me the happiest years of my life." About thirty minutes later, she said he spoke again: "Linda I trust you; please tell Dee that I want her to be happy." As Linda told me this, we heard birds chirping in the wall. It was a different room from where I had heard it before. Instinctively I shouted, "Marial, have you come back as Tweedy Bird?" At that very moment, his photo fell over and the CD skipped. Okay, that was enough evidence for both of us. Linda had channeled Marial, and his energy or spirit was in the room with us.

P.S. I could not have been happier!

Paranormal activity gets creative

The first week of October, I saw Marial. My bedroom was downstairs. My mom's and Marial's bedrooms were upstairs. It was about three o'clock in the morning when I woke to the sound of footsteps upstairs. The house has hardwood floors, and when Marial used to walk the hall, his steps were very loud. What I heard literally made me sit up in bed and take notice. He was there, standing at the end of my bed. I reached out, speechless. I tried to speak, but it was as if my vocal cords were paralyzed. He said nothing and then he was gone. I was not afraid, although my heart was pounding. I lay back down to try to take it all in and peacefully fell back to sleep. When I woke the next morning, I knew it had not been a dream.

The following weekend I had a new friend with neck pain over for a Reiki session and dinner. When I completed the session, Rosette was still on the table and asked me if I had birds in *that* room. She pointed down the hall to Marial's room. "No," I answered. "Why do you ask?"

"While you were working on me, I heard birds chirping in that room. It lasted about ten minutes." Now this was wild, because I did not hear a thing, but yes, I knew the source. It still made me laugh inside to think of big Marial as a bird!

One of the most touching paranormal events transpired at my workplace. I was treating a new patient when a phone call for me came in. It was Honda where his car was in for a repair. My patient overheard my end of the conversation. When I got off the phone she asked, "What was your son's name?" "Marial," I replied.

"Oh my God! That is my three-year-old's imaginary friend's name. My husband and I cannot figure out where she came up with that name, as we have never heard it before." My radar was already on full alert. I told her that in the Dinka culture, Marial is the name for a kind of ox.

"Oh my God; she named her doll Oxy."

"How long has your daughter had this friend?" I asked.

"A couple of months," she replied.

I just came out with it. "Your daughter's imaginary friend is an angel and is not imaginary at all." To my surprise she told me that she knew it was a spirit and went on to tell me that as a nursery school teacher she sees this all the time. A lot of kids see and talk to spirits. Well, how clever was Marial to find a child whose mother would become my patient and tell me this story? I cried tears of joy. It was more evidence that he was still with us and doing what he loved most, playing with children.

I had tried sharing these accounts with my mom but never got more than a blank stare. I wasn't sure if it was the dementia or her utter disbelief in anything that she could not touch, taste, see, or feel! In late October, I once again heard footsteps upstairs in the middle of the night. The next morning I matter-of-factly asked my mom, "Did you see Marial last night?" She replied that she'd dreamed that he was standing at the foot of her bed reaching his hand out for her. Of course, by now you know that I did not think it was a dream, but there was no point going down that road with Mom.

November was here, and I was going to have a normal morning checking my e-mail. Well, there was nothing normal about it. When my inbox opened, the first unread mail in bold was to me from Marial *dated April 2008*! My heart started pounding as I clicked on to see what it was. The sociology term paper he had written and I had edited on race was staring out me. Impossible, I thought. Immediately I clicked back to my inbox and it was gone, but I hadn't deleted it, so I tried to search for it, but it simply was not there. Wow! He sent me an e-mail! This was one of those times I pulled out my pendulum to ask, Marial, are you here? A positive spin was more confirmation. A few days later I was on a Web site and began to enter my e-mail address into the Web form, but as I typed, deeko, Mariel's e-mail address appeared in the blank space. It was really weird. On my second try, I successfully got deekonga typed in. Marial was very clever with the computer. Maybe he just missed mucking about with it!

I had received my Reiki master attunement the week before Marial died, August 21 to be exact. I began using this healing art form immediately at the clinic, where I worked for a doctor in his physical therapy department. One of the clinic's counselors, who I'll refer to as Jane, had introduced me to the practice of Reiki a year before. We had become friends, and as a result of my loss she gave me a beautiful necklace with a large turquoise pendant shaped like Africa. Little did I know that the positive feedback she was getting from the Reiki treatments I was doing with some of her patients was, shall we say, getting the best of her ego. One night, I came home from work wearing the necklace that she'd given me three weeks before when suddenly, without cause, it broke. Little beads scattered all over the living room floor and the big Africa turquoise pendant lay at my feet. My first reaction was, damn, I loved that necklace, but the meaning made itself crystal clear the next day. Shortly after lunch, Bennie called me into her office, shut the door, and informed me that the Director of Behavioral Services (Jane's big buddy, by the way) told her that I was not to do any more Reiki and that it was for Jane only. The decision had been made, and the head counselor would personally inform me soon. I was furious; Jane had thrown me under the bus, and guess what? Marial was not happy either. I know he broke that necklace! But he wasn't done. Two days later, I was called into the Director's office with Dr. Smith and I was coldly told I was not to do any more Reiki. Reiki was only to be practiced by the counseling department. What bullshit, I thought. Since when is it more appropriate for a counselor to lay her hands on a patient that someone in my field? I blurted out, "I know Jane put you up to this." He became enraged and then went after me for talking to the staff about Marial's presence. This was the last straw. "You are not going to take away my miracles from heaven," I said, and I got up and walked out. We soon broke for the Thanksgiving holiday. What was about to happen to little Evie, the Director of Behavioral Services, will make you laugh!

Thanksgiving was extremely painful; I literally cried all weekend. There was no one to cook for and no one to take out. The year before Marial, Mom, and I had gone to a beautiful hotel buffet and had a blast. The Monday following Thanksgiving marked the three-month anniversary of his death. I only worked at the clinic on Tuesday, Wednesday, and Thursday. It was raining and cold as I drove to the bank to make a deposit. Of course, the windows were rolled up, so how taken aback was I to find upon my return to the car a beautiful blond feather in the driver's seat. I have never seen a bird with this color. If there was ever a sense of knowing, this was it. In the midst of my sorrow and unbearable grief, Marial had given me a feather. It was a treasure like no other. I put it in secure place in my treatment room at home, where I was sure not to lose it. Now I had the strength to go back to work, reassured I was not alone.

Every Tuesday morning the professional providers met with Dr. Smith for a staffing of the patients. Little Evie, please forgive the sarcasm, but I never liked that man, came in bewildered. He announced that the very large and exquisitely decorated Christmas tree that he and his wife had put up had fallen over during the night without provocation, and a few books had "flown off the bookshelf." Bennie looked at me, and I knew what she was thinking. But surely Marial had not knocked over the tree. When it happened three nights in a row, there was no doubt in my mind. Marial was mad as hell that I was not allowed to do my healing work, and he was not going to let little Evie get away with it. In less than a month, Dr. Smith came to me and said to go ahead with my Reiki but to ask him to write a script first. I never heard another word from Jane or little Evie regarding Reiki. This, however, was only the beginning of Marial's ability to move and tamper with things!

It would seem that he was busy at my house, too. The same week Evie's tree was falling, my disposal, dishwasher and iPod stopped working, and my bedroom light went out even though the bulb was new. Frustrated, I called a friend to see if I could borrow her husband, who was quite handy. At the time, I did not know how to fix anything, as I would always go to my husband and subsequently to Marial, who could figure out literally anything. Well, Bert was not at my house five minutes before he got everything to work just fine. Was Marial trying to embarrass me? No, he was just being his old prankster self. There may have been a message too that I needed to be more self-sufficient and patient, as I was on my own now.

I had always slept on the right side of my bed, probably because it is closest to the bathroom. One night I woke up around three to find that my side of the bed was soaked. The sheets and the mattress were wet. My first thought was, Oh God, the dog has peed on my bed. Both dogs were asleep on the floor, so I got up to investigate. First I smelled it, and no it was not urine. I looked to the ceiling checking for a leak. No water there. To further complicate the mystery, my bedspread was not wet, but the sheets above and below me were. The other side was completely dry. This was a dilemma for my pendulum. Call me crazy, but I pulled it out and asked the burning question, "Marial did you do this?" I got a wild positive spin yes. I had to laugh, scratch my head, and ask myself how

I Will Never Leave You

he did it. Now I was wide awake, so I went to the bathroom and there was water all over the floor. It was not until later the next morning that I found water on his bathroom floor too. I shouted, "Okay funny boy, are you going to clean up now?" You guessed it, nothing happened. He never liked cleaning up!

Then things got a bit more serious. I had never given archangels much thought. Two weeks before Marial died, I did buy a little book on the Archangel Michael, but I have no idea why. It had a painting of his face on the front cover and some prayers inside. I was to learn that Marial's father was named Michael, and Marial's Christian name was Michael. His friends planned his funeral, which was held at Saint Michael and All Angels Episcopal Church. I presented the eulogy and read from my little book a passage describing the qualities of the Archangel Michael and compared them to Marial, who I described as an angel on earth. On November 27 I went into my meditation room to ask the Archangel Michael to be my guide and guardian. I suddenly looked down on the floor and found myself staring at a round, flat disc. It was a Christmas ornament with Michael's picture on it, the same picture that is on my little book. Two things struck me as strange. First,

The book and the Christmas ornament that I found on the floor.

all the Christmas ornaments were packed away in the garage, and second, I always thought that it was a picture of Jesus. I reached down to pick it up, and my white noise machine that was on continuous play just shut off. It was set on Rain Forrest, which provided the sound of birds chirping. Now it was not even a question of who was doing these things; I was comforted knowing that it was one of my angels. A bit shaken, I ran to another room where the little book was kept. I opened the book randomly and it fell upon a page wherein the name Gabriel and Michael were in the same sentence.

The hair on the back of my neck was standing straight up, but it was all good!

Every morning I put on a guided imagery CD to assist me in meditation. This practice took place in what I called my meditation room, which is where I had carefully placed my feather a couple of weeks before. To my horror, when I went in one Monday morning to meditate, the feather was not there. I looked high and low in a panic, even accusing my mother of throwing it away. Her response was, "I have not touched your damn feather." Okay then, where was it? I was really sick to my stomach because that "damn feather" had given me a lot of comfort. It was in fact a present from my deceased son.

Five days later, I found the feather lying on the floor of our front entrance hall. Impossible! I had been in and out of that door a dozen times in the last five days, and it had not been there or anywhere else for that matter. This time I got mad and yelled at him, saying something to the effect of if you want to let me know you are around, do not do it in a manner that is going to stress me out! To redeem himself, he played some trick with my computer printer later that day. I was trying to print a picture of beautiful purple flowers to put in a frame for my desk at work. I clicked the print button five times but the printer did nothing. Frustrated was not close to how I felt. Once again I yelled at him, "Okay Mike, I know you are messing with my printer, please make it work!" Suddenly the printer spit out a picture of Marial's face After it came through, I was able to successfully print my flowers and never had another problem with that printer. The most remarkable thing about his photo is that it has the *Mona Lisa* effect. I stuck it on a mirror on my wall, and no matter where in my room I would stand, his eyes seemed to follow me. I have never seen anything like it, except the *Mona Lisa*. The message was clear: he was looking out and over me, wherever I was.

Lower-back pain and I go way back, but fortunately, in the last five years or so, I had been doing well. In early December 2009, I had a back spasm that put me in bed. I have a theory that pain and illness are somehow connected to one's emotional wellbeing, so I concluded that my grief had gone to my most vulnerable area, my lower back. During the night I saw Marial. He had a really big, happy smile on his face and said, "I love you," kissed me on the cheek, and was gone. The next morning, I received a long-awaited e-mail from his brother that said he and his mom had made it to Kenya. In 2003, Marial learned that his mother was alive. She showed up at the very same refugee camp that he had been in. For years, he'd thought she was dead. Once she arrived in Kakuma, Kenya, he did talk to her for the first time since he was ten. Actually, he said they cried more than talked. Understandable. A few months later, through Deng's translation, the mother sent me an e-mail. First, she thanked me for putting her boys in school and how she wished she were not illiterate so that she could write this letter herself. The gut-wrenching message continued. She stated, "You are now Marial's mother, I give my son to you." Those are the most powerful words that have ever been spoken to me.

After he died, I was determined to meet his mother. The impossible was achieved. Deng, who was serving in the Sudanese Army, received a leave of absence; he then went to the village and got his mom. They traveled to the capital, Juba, to obtain travel documents. That alone took a month and a lot of money. Then there was the long journey to where I could meet them in Kenya. Deng was to e-mail me once they crossed the border so I could make my travel plans and go! Being so close to Christmas, air travel was much more expensive. I went online, and the first flight I found was $12,000. No way; I did not have that kind of money, so I called a travel agent. She could not find anything under $4,000. Shaking and crying, I went online again. A flight that connected in South Africa was $1,200. Perfect. I started to book and my computer crashed. More stressed than words can express, I had a meltdown. After waiting thirty minutes, I tried again, found the flight, got to the last step, and the page timed out. I couldn't believe this was happening. Deng and his mother had traveled over a thousand miles to see me, and I could not book an damn ticket! Suddenly, the page reappeared, I got my credit card number in, and it was done. I had a ticket. Understand, it was either divine intervention or Marial messing with numbers, because there is no way one can travel round-trip to Kenya for $1,200, not then or now, in the month of December.

First, I visited a medium for a reading

I had never been to a medium; I'd never had a reason. When I was told that there was a guy at a local bookstore that was really good, I thought I must give it a try. On December 13, 2009, I went to a man named Carl. I simply sat down and said nothing. The following is an account of what he said, according to the notes that I took.

"I see a contemporary, he had hard time breathing when he passed, he is holding the number five [Marial was the fifth child in his family to die and was buried on the fifth of September]. His death will lead to other things spiritually for you. He takes credit for that; you healed him so much, did so much for him, he says he will not have to repeat the same stuff. You were his angel, you will reincarnate together again on a soul level." Carl then begins to describe his energy as he sees it. "Pure heart, good shape, and he took pride in his appearance [Marial changed clothes three times a day]. He was loving and humble; he did not see in himself what you saw in him, and he is thanking you for that, old soul, God sent him to you, had no pain when he died, it was instant, went straight over, which is unusual for one who dies in a trauma. He is protecting you; you will be stronger as a result of his death, says he knocked over a tree!" At this point, Carl asked his first question, "Do you know what he is talking about?" Tears were pouring down my face. I knew I was communicating with Marial, so I could only nod my head yes. Carl then said my protector guide is something like Kalier. He told me to look it up, thinking it was Arabic and see what other name I got. When I Googled it, I found the name to be Gabriel! Everything Carl said about Marial was true. That session did more for me than a year of psychotherapy ever could have.

Warning! There are a lot more fakes out there than there are people as gifted as Carl, so please do your homework before paying anyone who says that he can channel.

My second trip to Africa

It was my strongest desire to meet Marial's mother and to take as many of his belongings as I could fit into two suitcases. On December 21, 2009, I took off on a very long journey—twenty-three hours, in fact, as there was an eight-hour layover in Johannesburg, South Africa. My plane arrived at 5:00 a.m., so I had  Deng check into the Hilton in Nairobi the day before so he could get some rest in a bed. It had been a while since he had experienced that luxury. It was so good to see him, but he looked terrible. He was so depressed over the loss of his brother and best friend that he just did not seem like the same man I had visited in 2004.

[The picture above quite literally appeared as I was writing. I in no way went to the documents where pictures are stored. I have over five hundred pictures on my computer, but how interesting it is that the only picture I have that includes both me and an orb should suddenly appear. This picture is #372; add those numbers together and you get 12. The meaning of that number will take on meaning in a future chapter. I'll get into more on orbs later, but the significance of this picture is that I was in Alabama visiting Dr. Raymond Moody, author of the bestselling book *Life after Life*, for a documentary that was being filmed by A&E network on the psychomanteum, a chamber for mirror gazing to contact the deceased. Just prior to my interview, I handed my camera to one of the film photographers and said, "Marial if you are here let us see you." In the mirror you can see an orb. It is very clear to me that while writing about going to visit his mom in Africa he pops in to say he is with me now, just as he did when the picture was taken. I really had to laugh out loud, thank him, and take a break from writing. Hours later when I came back to my computer, my photo had been downloaded into my manuscript. Unbelievable! He is undoubtedly trying to help me write this book.

{Note} After the above picture was mysteriously downloaded by spirit, the apparent electomagnetic field was so enormous that my computer contracted a very complicated virus that took days remove. My computer repair man is the best but he said he had never seen anything like it.

close up of orb in the mirror

Now I need to regain my story and tell you about seeing Deng again for the first time in five years.

First, I shared some of the stories with Deng about Marial coming to visit me from the other side and how much comfort I received from knowing that he was still around. When I asked Deng if he had seen Marial or experienced anything out of the ordinary, his reply was shocking. The week following Marial's death, Deng said he was contemplating suicide. Being in the army, he had a gun on him at all times. He said Marial appeared to him in a dream and said, "Don't go there." When he awoke the next morning, Deng had changed his mind about ending his life. I told him I didn't think it was a dream, and, from the look on his face, I don't think he did either.

The next day we took a bus to the town of Nakuru where I was to meet his mother and two young boys that had been born since my last visit. I was very nervous and didn't know what to expect. I was sitting by the pool at my hotel when I looked up and saw the family come through the lobby door. The mother was at least six feet tall with the most stoic look on her face. I greeted her first, and then the little boys, who I swear looked like a carbon copies of Marial. None of them could speak a word of English, so Deng had to translate my every bit of communication with them. The mother looked deep in my eyes, held my hand, and thanked me for putting her boy through school. I was in Kenya for five days but never, not once, did I ever see her smile. Through war, disease, and now a senseless accident, she had lost her fifth child. We did bond the way only mothers could. She held my hand as we walked the streets or just sat around the hotel room. I had taken so many pictures of Marial, but she refused to look at even one of them. I had left Atlanta with two large suitcases full of his clothes and shoes for Deng and relatives to have and many Christmas presents for the little boys and mother. Unfortunately, they went missing at the airport. I spent the first two days shopping for underwear and clothing and making countless calls to the airport, hotel, and everywhere else looking for my luggage. Every night after dinner, Deng would take the family to their little hut in the ghetto and return to the hotel to stay with me. There were two full-size beds each with a mosquito net around them. It was summer in that part of the world, so the first night I left the window open. Deng had one of his terrible nightmares. After going back to sleep, I heard very loud birds chirping, so loud that I got up and turned on the light, as I was sure they were in the room. I found nothing, but I did shut the window. It happened every night that I was in Africa, and the sound always came from right over Deng's bed. It was clear Marial was there to protect his brother. On my last night in Nakuru, I had the most amazing dream. There was a very large field of rolling hills literally carpeted in peacocks. I had no idea at the time what it meant, but it was the most beautiful sight I had ever seen. It was also a message from the other side that would soon take on great spiritual meaning.

The next morning I prepared a plastic bag with a few personal items for my journey home. I gave my carry-on and what clothes I had to Deng's wife, as my large luggage was still lost. It was Christmas Eve and everyone seemed to be going somewhere. Navigating the streets was even more dangerous than usual, and that is saying something. Deng held my hand and pulled me along dodging cars and trucks as we made our way to a park to meet up with his mom for a final good-bye and to take our last photos together. It was bittersweet, but I was so glad I had finally met the woman who had given Marial life.

Last picture taken with brother Deng and mother to Marial on Christmas 2009 in Kenya

Our two-hour bus trip back to Nairobi took over four hours due to the holiday traffic. Once at the airport, Deng and I went one more time to look for my luggage. This time we found it! No one had tampered with the suitcases, which was a miracle in itself. All the Christmas presents and clothes were there. It was one of the happiest moments of my life. Now Deng could return to Nakuru to spend Christmas with his family, distribute presents for all, and, most importantly, cherish his brother's possessions.

First picture taken of all of us the day I met Marial's mother and Deng's wife and boys.

Giving a gold necklace to his mother. From my heart to hers.

It was around 2:00 in the afternoon, and my plane did not leave until 9:00 that evening. There would be plenty of time to check in and assure myself a good seat so I could stretch out and sleep the eight hours to London. When I requested an aisle seat, the gate agent informed me that the plane was full and only a middle seat was available. There were so many hours to wait with nothing to do. The Nairobi airport does not have carpet or comfortable chairs, so sleeping was not an option. Believe me, by the time we were allowed to board, I was in desperate need of some rest. I took my middle seat next to a man to my right who was also on his way to the U.S. By the time the flight attendant started to prepare us for takeoff, I realized there was no one sitting to my left—a miracle of sorts. I turned to the gentleman to my right and asked if we could take turns lying across two seats to sleep. He replied that he was so excited about going to see his wife he did not want to sleep. I looked down at my ticket and saw my seat assignment was 46D. I was forty-six when Marial came to live with me, and my name is Dee. I *knew* Marial had somehow arranged that seat for me; it was all just too good to be true. Once the seat belt sign was off, I laid down and fell fast asleep.

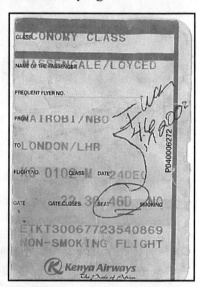

My ticket stub Seat 46D - I was 46 years old in 2002 when Marial came to live with us.

I finally reached Atlanta late on Christmas night where my dear Turkish friends collected me at the airport and took me back to their house for a dinner with my mother. I was surely the only international traveler, other than a refugee, to get off a plane with absolutely no luggage. I was happy to have left what I did behind and to come home to all that was left of my family, my mother.

On New Year's Eve, I booked another appointment with Carl, wanting to know how Marial felt about my trip to see his family. On that morning I went to my computer to check e-mail. In the midst of my reading my messages, Carl's picture overtook my screen. What the hell, I began hitting buttons trying to return to my mail when a beautiful picture of a peacock came on the screen. Now I knew spirit was trying to get my attention. I immediately went to Google and looked up the symbolism of the peacock. It is *immortality*! The hours leading up to my appointment with Carl seemed like days. When it finally arrived, I had decided not to tell him about any of this until the reading was over.

Many times as a medium begins, they get the sound or letter of the person's name that is coming through. Carl began by stuttering, "ba baa," and I was thinking no, his name doesn't have a B. At that, Carl blurted out, "Black, someone is coming through saying he is Black and "your car, my date." At that I began to cry, as Marial had died in my car hours after his birthday! I am saying nothing as Carl goes on, "He moves things around, and did he live in a hut? He has a sister with twins with no man around and that he says he needs to protect them [at the time I did not know her husband was in the army]. I see a horrific life, but Marial says he signed up for it, he is an enlightened being, not just a spirit, a real angel, brought into this world in part to change you. He says you talk to him a lot." Carl gently places his hands together and says things are coming together—he sees a big smile, a soft touch, and gentle spirit. He tells me that Marial spends a lot of time with my mom trying to help her pass. Marial says I need to get a plan and that it would be a year of smiles and growing.

"You had asked him to come back and he has," Carl said. I was really blown away by that. Then Carl repeated, "He had a hard physical life, but he came to learn and says he gained so much more spiritually than he lost and that he chose this. He says to let you know he is not putting himself with Jesus and that he gained more than he lost." I still don't understand what the Jesus comment means. The channeling was so fast, rarely in complete sentences. Carl just spat out what he got, and

I scribbled it down. When time was up, I had to ask, "Carl, did you put your picture on my computer screen this morning?"

"No," he shouted, then he looked up and then back at me, stating, "He said he did it."

"Do you know what the deal is with the peacock," I queried?

"Look behind you."

When I turned around, I saw a vase with at least fifty peacock feathers in it. I also noticed that on one wall, there hung a beautiful oil painting of two peacocks. Marial must have been excited about my appointment with Carl, as he knew he would really be able to communicate with me. I left that reading feeling an enormous peace even though nothing was said about my visit to Africa. I knew in my heart it had meant a lot to his brother and mother, so no other conformation was really needed.

NOTE: Carl rarely asks questions, and I am careful never to give a psychic any information. All that he says comes from his or my guides and the spirits that he channels.

2010 Year of the Ox

Some friends joined me New Year's Day for lunch at a Chinese restaurant. How shocked was I to learn that it was the year of the Ox? Remember, Marial is the name of an Ox in Dinka. Was this a coincidence, synchronicity, or a foretelling of the truth? *It turned out to be all of the above.*

On January 7, I cleaned out his closet, bagged all his clothes, and called James to come and pick them up. I had bought him everything he had, and it just made me sad to see the clothes go. After he left I went into my meditation room at 2:22 to clean and found that the water from my little fountain had somehow shot over to the adjacent orchid and filled the container to the top, but not one drop of water was on the table in between the fountain and the flowers. Oddly, the clock still read 2:22. There is no other word than the one I have used over and over: *impossible!* Remarkably, all that water did not have a negative effect on the orchids, which require little to no water. On January 8, a high school friend named Bobbie that I had not seen in years came for Reiki. She was flying to Japan the next day, but she had a lot of back pain and was desperate for a quick fix. Just before she rang the doorbell, I noticed that the fountain was dry and the water was in the plant. I ran to fill up a glass of water to put in the fountain but answered the door first. We hugged and had our initial greetings. Then I went straight into the Reiki treatment room where I poured the water into the fountain. This time, the water squirted straight up and went all over the window. I was shaking and didn't know what to say to her, so I just came out with it: "Marial has been playing with my water fountain tonight. I hope you don't mind." Little did I know it, but Bobbie was very connected to spirit; if she hadn't been, she might never have returned! Bobbie immediately noticed the Archangel Michael disc that I had above the massage table and told me he was her patron saint. "I will ask him to assist in our healing session," I told her. From my perspective the hour

was normal but what Bobbie had to share was nothing short of remarkable. She said she saw Marial, that he looked to be about four years old with a big smile and a childlike manner (which describes him to a tee). The impression she got was that he was rubbing up against my leg like a cat. "Your souls are entwined as one," she said. I was speechless, because she knew nothing about him or anything I had experienced since his death. When we were in high school we had never talked about such things. I had to ask if she had become psychic. Humbly, she described having a shared near-death experience with her son when he was eighteen. He had been struck by a car and suffered serious head injuries. She got the news while out of town. Frantically trying to get to an airport, she saw him in the light and knew he must be dead. It was over a year before her boy was out of a coma and had learned to talk again that he shared with her the same experience that she'd had on the way to the airport. I have read over and over that near-death experiences, going through the tunnel and into the light, have profound spiritual effects on the survivor. We talked for hours about these things, and it was truly such a blessing. I am sure I healed more that evening from listening than she did from the energy work.

Messages start to come in numbers

To add to my challenge of dealing with my grief without the support of a significant other, sibling, or child, I was taking care of my mother, whose dementia seemed to get worse by the day. I tried hiring sitters, but she fired them. Coming home from work was often like entering a house of horrors. I never knew what I was going to find. If she were cold, the thermostat would be on ninety and the oven door open and set on four hundred and fifty. Frequently she could not remember how to cut off the shower, and hot water might run for the nine to ten hours while I was away. This left the upstairs looking and feeling like a steam room at the gym. Sometimes the front door was open, and the dogs escaped. You get the picture—it was nerve-racking and challenging to say the least. I had become rather fixated on trying to figure out how long this may go on. It is not that I wanted her to die; I just wanted to escape the madness. Assisted living was out of the question. "I am going to die in this house," she would say.

Sadly, since my marriage in 1994, my mother's and my relationship had deteriorated. My husband and Mom could not stand the other and put me in the middle. She really was rude to him, and he was eventually rude to her. Mom had her first stroke only one year after I married, and I made the decision to move back to Atlanta from England to take care of her. My husband followed six months later, but things were never the same. I always blamed my mom for the demise of my marriage, but in retrospect that is unfair. All three of us were to blame. My husband became mean as a snake and was emotionally abusive to me. Every day I thought it would get better because it could not get any worse. When Marial moved in, he was very disturbed by what he saw. He came to me one day and said he didn't like that Trevor made me cry every day. Shortly after that, Trevor started to treat Marial the same way. That is when I put my foot down. I told Trevor, "It is one thing for you to treat me like shit, but over my dead body are you going to do or say anything to belittle Gabriel. I do not love you anymore; get out of my house." It was the best move I ever made, but I could never have done it for me. I did it for Marial. My need to protect him gave me strength. Marial had only lived with us for three months when this happened. Immediately after Trevor left, things started to get better with my mom, but we had a long way to go. She had been in a constant state of anger at my husband, and it was time for all to chill. Every day after school, Marial would go straight to my mom's TV room where she would be watching CNN. They would talk politics, and he would often offer to drive her to the market to buy ice cream. I never minded him borrowing my car, especially if it meant I got out of having to take her shopping. A three-item list could often take two hours. I did not have the patience. He did. They grew very close, and it was not long before she clearly enjoyed his company more than mine. His very presence was healing to both of us.

The month of January was filled with daily happenings—small hellos from heaven. For example, on January 12, his picture, which I kept in my calendar book downstairs, appeared on the floor by my massage table after I had done my morning meditation. It definitely was not there when I had entered the room thirty minutes earlier. In the early morning hours of January 13, I felt "something" sit on the end of my bed by my feet. On January 14, all the water from my fountain had emptied into the adjacent plant, but when I went to refill it, water exploded all over the window. Instead of the water just draining into the empty fountain, it formed a reverse waterfall. He was busy on January 16. Water moved out of my fountain to the plant again just before a client arrived for Reiki. I refilled it as she was ringing the doorbell. During our session, it happened again! It was hard to keep my focus, and I waited until the end to tell her. (This client was intrigued by my stories.) She informed me that she had felt something tickling her foot while my hands were on her back. This young girl is very beautiful, so it made me laugh to think of Marial flirting with her, but he was not finished. I looked down and there was a small feather on my foot, and the original feather that I had found after Thanksgiving had moved to the opposite side of the table where I had it secured under a rock. It was comforting to know that he was with me while I was doing my healing work, as I always pray before a session that God and the angels will help me. On the following day, Rick and his lovely wife Janet came over to look at my photos from the trip to Africa. We sat on my living room sofa, and I told them all about Marial's mother, brother, and precious nephews. When the viewing was complete, we all stood up and at that very moment we heard birds chirping in the wall. It was a surreal moment, as we all knew he was with us. I then took them into my meditation/Reiki room to show them the feather. At that point, my white noise machine was always on playing sounds from the rain forest, which included bird chirping, so when we entered that room and Rick once again heard a bird, he turned white as a sheet. I burst out laughing and assured him this time it was the machine!

Finding pennies in unlikely places happened so often that I will not record all of those incidents here, but they continue to bring a smile to my face all the same. As a child I had a book entitled *Pennies from Heaven*. Apparently, dropping pennies is easy for our spirit loved ones to do.

Close friends were aware of the bird connection to Marial. For

Christmas, my Turkish friend Zekia gave me two ceramic doves that I kept on a small table in the meditation room. In February, the disastrous earthquake hit Haiti. Bennie's husband was in the National Guard and was called to go and serve. Needless to say, Bennie was worried sick. Would there be more aftershocks? Would he forever be traumatized by witnessing such suffering? In my attempts to comfort her, I took one of my doves to work and slipped it into her very large purse with a note saying that I had asked Marial to protect her husband and when she looks at the dove, know that he is protected by an angel. What happened on February 22, 2010 even surprised me. Bennie and a psychologist friend had set up a Skype conference call with her husband's commanding officer to advise him on PTSD-prevention strategies. Both Bennie and her husband are looking at their laptop screens awaiting the officer when, lo and behold, the screen goes blank and a large picture of a dove appears on both computers. As she recounted the story, both she and her husband blurt out "Marial!" She says the picture was on the screen for approximately twenty seconds. A few days later, her husband suffered symptoms of a kidney stone and was sent back home. This really was a blessing in disguise because at age forty-six and overweight, he was not up to the task at hand in Haiti. Remember back in early January when my clock got stuck on 2:22? Was Marial trying to tell me that he was going to show us his presence in a big way on 2/22? Well you know what I think! The next day at work, one of my patients brought me some feathers. She owns fourteen exotic birds. I asked her why she had thought to bring me feathers and she simply replied, "I don't know." At this I proclaimed that I wanted a dove. "No problem. Mine mate, and I have to throw out the eggs every month. In three months I should have two doves for you." It ended up taking a little longer, but on May 22 I received my two baby birds.

Protection

Do not be fooled; although I received continual communication from the other side, my grief was still very raw, very real. Marial was not just like a son, he was my best friend, my big brother, my uncle; he was my family and the only family at that. Mom's dementia had taken her away from me. The first year after losing him I got into a very bad habit of locking myself in my room at night with a bottle of wine and would scream, "Come back." He took care of that craziness in a remarkable way. I will discuss that miracle in the chapter Healing from the Other Side.

It was now February and a very real symptom of my grief was playing out over and over: memory loss. I had been driving Marial's hybrid Honda and, unlike my foolproof car that he totaled, you have to remember to cut off the lights. Two nights in one week I came home from work, put the car in the garage, and failed to turn the lights off. Waking up on a cold winter's morning to a dead battery is annoying enough, but with the hybrid, once the battery died the clock and the radio went out too. I would have to drive to the dealer to have them reset the clock. Never mind how annoyed my neighbor must have been when I rang the doorbell at 7:30 a.m. to ask him to jumpstart my car. Actually, after it happened the second time, Bo lent me his portable cable starter, just in case. Apparently my disturbed energy field was obvious. Sure enough, the very next week I did it again. No problem, I thought. I have the charger so I can do this, but it did mean another trip to Honda to have the clock and radio turned back on. To my utter amazement, as I was pulling out of my driveway I noticed the clock was on, set to the correct time and the radio was playing too! Impossible; I mean impossible! It turned out that it was more than a sign that he was with me that morning. About one mile from work I made a left turn through heavy, fast oncoming traffic. Thirty seconds later, the car died in a very safe, quiet place. I truly believe that Marial got me through that intersection. If the car had died moments before, I would have been hit. Turned out the radiator had a hole in it and the car over heated. Maybe the dead battery was Marial trying to prevent me from driving, as I would have eventually seen the radiator fluid on driveway. The next morning when I was selecting my angel card, a photo of Marial appeared stuck to the card that read, "Archangel Michael is protecting you." Was this a coincidence? I don't think so!

Personality and temperament do not change in spirit

One morning I received a call from my friend Fred who has always been interested in the paranormal. He had just listened to a radio interview with a woman who claimed to be a psychic and suggested I check out her Web site. I must admit it was the most impressive site I have ever seen; it was like a trip to another planet. Intrigued, I called her and was able to make an appointment for the following day. The next morning while anxiously awaiting my appointment, I pulled my angel cards and got "Hello from Heaven" and "You are Safe and Protected." Perfect, I thought. However, the first red flag went up when I arrived at her lovely home. She came to the door looking like she had just gotten out of bed. Her hair was a mess and she was wearing sweatpants and a T-shirt. Who would greet a client like that? The first thing she asked me was my birth date and time. She entered the information into her computer to run an astrological chart. I had not asked for this, nor did I have any interest in it. By the time she had gone over it with me, a good hour was up and I was on the clock, but as far as I was concerned we had not started yet. I politely asked if we could get on with the reading. A dozen questions were fired at me. What authentic psychic asks questions? Once she learned of my loss and the circumstances around it, she told me that it was my fault that he had the accident since I had placed the 1:30 a.m. call. She also told me that he was not my guardian angel and not any kind of highly evolved spirit. At that, I got up and walked toward the door. The nutcase, who we will call Ms M., chased me, yelling, "Aren't you going to pay me?" I threw some money on her table (which I regret) and walked out. Her last words to me were, "Well, don't have a wreck."

To say I was shaking all over is an understatement. As it turns out Marial was every bit as upset as I was. When I arrived home my bedroom looked like a tornado had hit. My DVD player had come off its shelf and was on the floor. Lying next to it was an overturned pencil holder, a black feather, a penny, and a business card that had a picture of a dove on it. My throw pillows were also in the middle of my floor. The message was loud and clear. Marial was saying to me that it was not my fault and Ms M. was a crackpot! I rarely ever saw Marial get mad, but when he did it was a quiet rage that one could see in his eyes. I had witnessed it a few times when my husband was tormenting me, and Marial had walked in on it. Just to make sure I got the message, the scene was repeated the next morning. I woke up to find the DVD player once again on my floor amid scattered pillows the feather, penny, and card. It was another *wow* moment. I felt reassured that I was being heard, watched, and protected.

If Marial knocked over little Evie's tree, I wonder what he did to Ms. M.?

The obvious moral to this story is that you must do your homework, get references, or only go to a medium or psychic that you can verify is authentic.

On the night following this horrible ordeal, I had the loveliest dream that seemed so real. I was simply on the telephone having a delightful conversation with Marial, just like we had done so many times before. When I woke up, I was disappointed that it was a dream, but I was soon made to smile again. My feather had been moved and there was water all over my bathroom floor. You are probably thinking that I needed to call a plumber. No worries; my pipes are fine.

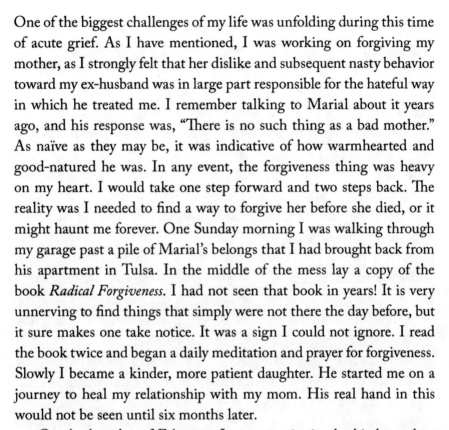

One of the biggest challenges of my life was unfolding during this time of acute grief. As I have mentioned, I was working on forgiving my mother, as I strongly felt that her dislike and subsequent nasty behavior toward my ex-husband was in large part responsible for the hateful way in which he treated me. I remember talking to Marial about it years ago, and his response was, "There is no such thing as a bad mother." As naïve as they may be, it was indicative of how warmhearted and good-natured he was. In any event, the forgiveness thing was heavy on my heart. I would take one step forward and two steps back. The reality was I needed to find a way to forgive her before she died, or it might haunt me forever. One Sunday morning I was walking through my garage past a pile of Marial's belongs that I had brought back from his apartment in Tulsa. In the middle of the mess lay a copy of the book *Radical Forgiveness*. I had not seen that book in years! It is very unnerving to find things that simply were not there the day before, but it sure makes one take notice. It was a sign I could not ignore. I read the book twice and began a daily meditation and prayer for forgiveness. Slowly I became a kinder, more patient daughter. He started me on a journey to heal my relationship with my mom. His real hand in this would not be seen until six months later.

On the last day of February, I was upstairs in the kitchen when suddenly my CD player in my room came on, really loud. I immediately ran down the stairs and of course no one was there, so I knew that Marial had done this. At this point, I did not know if I should try to talk to him, dance, sing, laugh, or just leave the music on and resume my cooking. I did the latter. He was not finished; when I went back upstairs my bedroom door was locked, which, as I have mentioned, has to be done by turning the lock, which I definitely did not do. In fact, I did not even shut my door when I ran down to check on the music. Happy morning; I was not alone.

Rev. Dee Massengale, DD, M.Ed, MA

More medium readings

It is now my third month in a class called Psychic Development with medium Carl Woodall. We meet all day Saturday and Sunday once a month; each class focuses on different skills. Most everyone in my class came to it knowing they had an obvious ability, but I was there just to learn more and try to have a better understanding about what and why so many unexplained things were happening in my house. It was also very comforting to be around other people who were open and sensitive to spirit and with whom I could share my stories without judgment. There was one unique lady I will refer to as Ms T. She was there to learn how to undo her abilities. Ever since she was a child she could hear and see dead people, and she hated it. Spirits would just pop in at unexpected times, and it was very disruptive to her. Carl taught us some methods to protect ourselves from that, and he did share some ways that she could tell the spirit to please leave her alone. We did not get to channeling until our fifth month, but that did not stop Marial from contacting Ms. T. He must have seen that it would be easy for him to give her a message for me. Late one night, Ms. T. left me a voice mail telling me that she was unable to sleep and that Marial had come through so strong and had urged her to tell me that although he did not want to leave me, he was where he needed to be. She continued that the strongest message was that he could protect me better from where he was than he could here on earth. He also said that he appreciated everything I had done for him and that he felt more centered now. Ms. T. emphasized the message of protection one more time, stating it was so strong that she even felt that she was protected too. There was no way she could have known any of this, as she knew nothing of my relationship with Marial. I never paid her for this, nor did I ask her to channel. It was a very authentic message in every way. Marial simply recognized that Ms. T. was an easy portal to me and used her to express his feelings.

Later in March, I had yet another apparition. Around 3:00 a.m. I heard a lot of movement upstairs. I sensed heavy energy moving around.

My dog, Dinkbear, began to cry, so I sat up to see what was wrong with her. The dog was on the floor at the foot of my bed and beside her stood Marial, who was wearing a bright blue shirt brushing his teeth. I have yet to figure out what that was about. He then smiled and said, "I love you" before he slowly disappeared. Once again, I heard heavy footsteps upstairs going toward my mom's room. As if to follow him, I jumped out of bed, but before I could reach the hallway, my bedroom door shut. At that, I got a little spooked and returned to bed. Believe it or not, I was able to go back to sleep. After each apparition I've seen, I feel a sense of peace that makes falling back to sleep easy.

The next morning, I went straight to my angel cards, and the first card I pulled was "Hello from Heaven." My feather had been moved, and there was a penny in its place. It really was a little more than I could process, but on the heels of the message from Ms. T., I indeed felt protected and more convinced than ever that Marial was still with me. Remember, he had once told me, "I will never leave you."

Every day in the week after the apparition, something unusual happened. Fortunately, I had been keeping a journal or it would not have been possible to remember all of this. The following is a list of what I deem to be more visitations.

My bed sheets were wet again and it is worth repeating there was no urine smell, so I could not blame my dog. My dryer would not come on but was not broken; my sauna went off while I was in it, and that had never happened in the ten years I have had it, nor has it happened since. My pencil holder fell over and the pens were all over the floor; I pulled "Hello from Heaven" three days in a row and found four pennies in four obscure locations all in one morning, I also found a little angel token I had given Marial years ago that had "Peace Be with You" engraved on it. I had not seen that token in years, and it just appeared in my sock drawer. The rain forest bird chirping on my white noise machine turned off two days in a row, even though it was always set on continuous play. While vacuuming, I came across a black fossil shaped like Africa that we had found while hiking in Oklahoma. I have no idea where it has been all this time. A little white feather shaped like an angel's wings appeared on my shoulder the morning of Carl's class. While writing in my journal about all this, the light went off in my sauna. Annoyed, I yelled "Mike" and the light came back on! Finally in Carl's class we were learning the art of crystal gazing. After a few minutes, I saw a Black man standing shoulder to shoulder with the Archangel Michael. Just think about the odds of seeing a Black man in a clear quartz crystal. You may be thinking this was just my imagination, but even if it was … it was comforting all the same!

My birthday is March 28. I was not looking forward to it because Marial, Mom, and I would always go out for a dinner celebration. On that morning, my mom and I were having a heated argument over her tax returns. I had recently learned that since her only income came from social security, she did not earn enough money to file. All these years she had been paying a CPA $200 to prepare her return, and it infuriated me that she was taken advantage of like that. I hid her tax envelope under the sofa so that she could not send it to her CPA. As hard as I tried, I could not convince her that I was telling the truth. She insisted I find her return and put it in the mail. I was mad, frustrated, and just plain exasperated, but I gave in. When I crawled under the sofa and reached for the envelope, to my delight I found a big, beautiful red feather sitting on it. It was my birthday present from Marial! How do I know that? Because I have never seen that feather in this house in my life! My mood went from miserable to ecstatic in a moment. He knew just how to make my day. Instead of going out to dinner, I decided to go to my favorite metaphysical book store and buy myself a present. In recent months I had become very interested in Shamanism and Native American lore, so it was no surprise that once in the store I gravitated toward a section with animal totem cards. My angel cards had brought a lot of insight and joy, so it seemed a good idea to learn more about the symbolism of animals. Once home, I shuffled the cards and asked my guides to show me my animal totem. Would you believe that I pulled the Wolf … the Protector!

Protection came through loud and clear on April 4. In life, Marial was like a nagging mother when it came to seeing that I locked the French doors that opened from my bedroom onto the patio. Every night after I had gone to sleep, he would come downstairs to check my doors.

This was due to my habit of leaving them open for fresh air and so the dogs could go out without waking me. He also had an issue about my bathroom window, which I liked to keep open. Being on the ground floor, he was worried that someone could break in and hurt me. Well, it was a beautiful and warm spring morning, so I opened my bathroom window and went upstairs to cook some breakfast. No sooner had I pulled out the eggs than my cell phone, which was in my bedroom began to ring. To my alarm, the door from the kitchen that goes downstairs to my room was locked. That should have been impossible because one has to turn the lock from the other side to lock that door. Nevertheless, I could not get downstairs. In somewhat of a startled panic I ran outside and down the driveway, hoping I had left the French doors unlocked so I could get back into my room and have access to my car. The doors were locked. Trying to figure out how I was going to break in, I noticed my bathroom window was open. I pulled a patio chair to the window, climbed up, and slithered feet first through the window, almost landing in my toilet. Oh God, that was easy enough that it convinced me if I could do it, so could the boogeyman. The message was deafening. Okay, Marial, I swear I will never open that window again!

A few days later, a patient brought me a copy of a book titled, *Journey of the Soul*. Initially, I found it intriguing, but it eventually got a little too weird, even for me. I had stayed up until 2:00 a.m. reading when I finally fell asleep. The next morning, the book was not on my bed; in fact, it was nowhere to be found. As off this writing, two years later, I have still not located the book. I thought then, as I believe now, that his spirit did not feel the information in that book was what I needed. Since my patient had lent me her copy, I was obliged to buy her a new one. This was the first of many things to disappear, but it was the only item that never reappeared. I was not even tempted to try to read a page of the new copy. I was learning that when spirit speaks, you are a fool not to listen.

On April 10, I once again heard footsteps in the middle of the night going from the kitchen to Mom's room. The next morning she announced, "I saw Marial last night." Mom did not elaborate, and I did not press. I was certain he was trying to help her pass, which just made the daily agony of wondering when she was going to die all the more intense. My biggest fear was that I was going to walk into her room one morning and find her dead, leaving me alone in every sense of the word.

That weekend I would be back in class with Carl and my new friends again. I really looked forward to my classes with Carl; they always took my mind away from my sorrows. That weekend, he was going to teach us how to channel. Totally convinced that I would never be able to do it, my excitement lay in the hope that someone else in the class would channel Marial for me. My wish was fulfilled. We were "forced" to practice gallery style, which means each student had to stand in front of everyone, go up into channel, and first simply see who they were drawn toward and then try to decipher who was coming through. One of the first students to volunteer was pulled to me. She never opened her eyes, so she really had no idea she was standing in front of me. The student stated there was a very tall, Black man wearing black pants and a blue shirt, holding a dove. The second she said "dove," I started to cry. His message was that, "He will be with your mom when she passes." The following day another student stood before me. She said she saw a man with open hands, saying, "I fulfilled my destiny, smoothed the edges." That was all she got, but it was enough for me.

To my surprise, I was able to channel too. I was pulled to a woman with my eyes closed. When I opened them, I told her I saw an old man in a wheelchair. He would not look up, so I did not see his eyes. I described a very rural farm area and a little house with a screen door. He told me to tell her that he was sorry. As soon as I said that, she got up and ran out of the room. Carl went after her, and they were gone for at least fifteen minutes. When she finally returned, she was visibly upset. I later learned that I had channeled her grandfather who had abused her. I felt so bad about this that I refused to pursue channeling. I decided to leave it to the experts. It would be over a year before I was emotionally grounded enough to take on that kind of responsibility anyway. I was, in fact, way overdue for receiving some Reiki. Carl told me about a new Reiki master who was very intuitive and had just started at the bookstore. Her fee was $45 more than I charge, so I was a bit hesitant. Well, I did make that appointment, and it was well worth it. Her name was Jackie, a very devout Catholic who started the session with a prayer and a sprinkling of holy water. I had never met her before, and she knew nothing about me. Once she laid her hands on my head she said, "There is a very tall Black man standing down by your feet. He is wearing a bright blue plaid shirt [Marial had one]. He kisses you on the forehead every night and never leaves you." At this she changed gears and said, "That is odd because spirits usually come and go, but this one is with you all the time." She told me his words, "Tell her to stop grieving." A little later in the session, she spoke of some of my guides that she could see and told me some interesting things about them. When I do Reiki, I rarely say a word so I don't lose my focus and intent. To say the least, it was a very interesting session that worked on multiple layers.

The week that followed was filled with events. For example, picture frames fell over; a shoe moved; a clock somehow unplugged itself; a plant fell to the floor from an end table and yes, left dirt all over the rug; my fully charged cell phone went dead during a call; my bedroom door opened to the kitchen in the middle of the night and then shut itself; there was water all over his bathroom floor *again*. But this next experience really stunned me. I went into my room at 1:47 p.m. to meditate, which takes about thirty minutes. When I got up to leave the clock read 12:22. When is the last time your clock went in reverse? It was a sign regarding the number 12; I had no idea what it meant at the time. Seven months later in the month of December (12), my mom had a stroke. She was hospitalized in room 222 and died on 2/1/2011 in room 12 in hospice.

It has now been eight months since Marial's passing. If you have ever lost anyone close, you know that the first year is full of wild mood swings. One minute you are fine and the next, a sadness sweeps over you that can knock you to your knees. You constantly have to create a new normal, and the fact is that the only thing that is normal is that you feel like you are losing your mind. That's right: if you think you are losing your mind, it's normal! Crazy people never stop and ask that question. Often in those moments, when I was in the midst of a sad meltdown or just plain missing him, something odd would happen, like the clock coming unplugged. I was having a very bad day early on in May when I went into the meditation room to once again find the clock unplugged. I inserted the plug, reset the time, and reached for my pendulum. "Am I crazy, or did Marial unplug the clock?" Before the pendulum had time to swing, the plug came out of the wall before my very eyes. This was not a loose socket! It never happened again.

On Mother's Day, I took flowers to place on Marial's grave. As I was ready to walk back to my car, I looked down, and there at my feet was the most beautiful fuchsia-colored feather I have ever seen. It was my Mother's Day present. I used to get a card, but this year I got a present. I simply looked up at the sky and said joyfully, "Thank you." Upon my return home, the CD clock radio in my room, which had been broken for months, started playing. It just spontaneously came on! Music and the miracle of Mariale.

The single happiest day of Marial's life while he was with me was the day he graduated from high school in 2006. He worked damn hard for that diploma and deserved to be proud. The ceremony was held at the Civic Center in downtown Atlanta. Afterward, I took Marial and a few of his friends to dinner at the top of the Peachtree Plaza hotel. It was truly an evening to remember. It is now May 2010, and his cousin David is scheduled to graduate in the same Civic Center. In spirit, Marial must have known that the evening was going to be a bittersweet one for me. For what ensued in the hours leading up to that graduation still blows my mind.

I Will Never Leave You

The happiest moment of Marial's life. The Atlantic Civic Center May 2006

After my morning coffee, I reached for my cell phone to call David and inquire what time I was to pick up his mom and siblings to take them to the Civic Center. My cell phone was dead, but as I reached for the charger, the phone rang! It was David calling to ask me to pick up his family at 4:00. How did a dead phone ring? Or is that a rhetorical question at this point? I checked my e-mail around 11:00 then took my dogs for a thirty-minute walk. At 1:30, I checked my e-mail again, but what I found still astounds me. There were three e-mails from Postmaster Return and marked 11:11 a.m., 5/21/10. The first was one that I had sent to Bennie six months prior that contained the lyrics to "The Impossible Dream." I had said to her that the song told Marial's story. The second e-mail contained photos of Marial's young nephews that I support in Kenya. This e-mail had been sent to his close friend and relative three months before. Both of these e-mails had been successfully received months ago, so it is *impossible* that they would turn up as returned. And finally, the third e-mail was that picture of me with the purple flowers in the background; the same picture that mysteriously appeared in my purse on the Tulsa trip; the same photo I used on my Web site when Barbara and I heard the chirping in the wall. This e-mail said it was sent by DEE. I don't even know how to do that, and as God as my witness, I did not do it. Please understand that I could not make this stuff up. I am simply not that creative!

>Impossible Dream
>
>To dream the impossible dream
>To fight the unbeatable foe
>To bear with unbearable sorrow
>To run where the brave dare not go
>
>(go on-line for full lyrics)

From: dee massenga;e (deekonga@bellsouth.net)   *I DID not do this*
To: deekonga@bellsouth.net;
Date: Fri, May 21, 2010 11:17:27 AM
Cc:
Subject: Emailing: Dee Pix 134

The message is ready to be sent with the following file or link attachments:

Dee Pix 134

Note: To protect against computer viruses, e-mail programs may prevent sending or receiving certain types of file attachments. Check your e-mail security settings to determine how attachments are handled.

Pix 134 is on page 118

Note: When writing this book + searching my email to print these, the one of the children's photos was listed but when I went to print it it disappeared.

From: postmaster@isp.att.net (postmaster@isp.att.net)
To: deekonga@bellsouth.net;
Date: Fri, May 21, 2010 11:18:09 AM
Cc:
Subject: Returned mail: delivery problems encountered

Note: Forwarded message is attached.

A message (from <deekonga@bellsouth.net>) was received at 21 May 2010 15:18:05 +0000.

The following addresses had delivery problems:

<____s@yahoo.com>
   Permanent Failure: MAIL FROM: <deekonga@bellsouth.net> 554 REPLY: 554_delivery_error:_dd_This_user_doesn't_have_a_yahoo.com_account_(____s@yahoo.com) [0]_-_mta1007.mail.sk1.yahoo.com
   Delivery last attempted at Fri, 21 May 2010 15:18:08 -0000

This e-mail was received by my friend 8 months prior!

Rev. Dee Massengale, DD, M.Ed, MA

I am not the only one who has seen Marial!

The first week in June, I took David's eight-year-old twin brothers to the mountains in north Georgia. We took a train ride, looked for waterfalls, played in a large hot tub, rented a cabin, and just had a great time. This family of twins, David, their sixteen-year-old sister and mom had been resettled to Atlanta from a refugee camp in Ethiopia in 2006. Marial was somehow related to the husband of Rachel, who is the children's mother. I know it sounds complicated, but in Sudanese culture, if you are even remotely related you take care of one another as you would your blood brother. This is no doubt a survival skill, but it's heartening all the same. When this family arrived back in 2006, Marial was over at their apartment helping in every way possible. It seemed he was the self-appointed uncle to look after this family. When they were awarded a Habitat for Humanity house in 2008, he worked on construction every weekend. During the summer months, Marial and I would take the kids to my neighborhood pool and try to teach them to swim. I have mentioned Marial loved playing with kids, and no doubt the twins, Monykuoch and Athiey loved him too!

We were driving south on Interstate I–85 when Monykuoch asked me how the hybrid battery in the car worked. Clueless, I just laughed and responded that Marial knew all that stuff, and I was sure he had discussed it with James. "Just ask him about it next time you see him," I said.

His answer to that almost made me run off the road. Out of his eight-year-old mouth came, "That's okay; I will ask Marial next time I see him in spirit."

Gripping the steering wheel tight, I responded, "Oh you see him when you are asleep?"

"Well I see him day and night. I especially like going there, and I like it better in the spirit world."

I then asked him about what Marial said to him and how long they'd been communicating. Monykuoch answered that the night after

Marial died, he saw him. Marial told him, "I will always be with all of you. Do not worry; I am okay." Athiey piped in and said the next morning his brother told him all of this and that they were both pretty freaked out. They never told their siblings or mom for fear they would not be believed. Although I do not recall mentioning any of my miracles from heaven to them, I must have said something that weekend that opened the door. To this day, I do not know where Monykuoch came up with the term "spirit world."

About a week later, I took the kids back to my neighborhood pool for another swimming lesson. It seemed a good time to ask the burning question to Monykuoch, "Have you seen Marial this week?"

"Yes."

"Well what did he say?"

He responded, "Be careful, he is always telling me to be careful so I do not get hurt. I was at a friend's house jumping on a trampoline, and Marial told me not to do a backflip because I would get hurt." It is worth noting here that Monykoush is quite the daredevil. He wants to swim in the deep end, but he cannot swim. Get the picture?

Thrilled that I had found someone who was also experiencing joy and healing from the other side, I felt compelled to make a request. As I dropped the kids back home I asked Monykuoch a favor. "Hey, the next time you see Marial, will you ask him to come and see me?" What happened next is really weird. The following night I had a horrible nightmare. It is only one of the two the dreams I have had that involved Marial that was not uplifting. It must have simply been my subconscious at work and not spirit intervention. In my dream, I received a call from a Tulsa hospital. The nurse said that Marial had been in a terrible accident and was in a coma. The doctors had performed multiple organ transplants over the last ten months, but he was not responding. My heart was racing and I was frantic to get to the hospital. Of course dreams jump around, so the next thing I knew I was on an airplane, which was experiencing the worst possible turbulence.

I was being thrown from one end of the plane to the other. Then the plane started spinning, and I knew it was going to crash. The fear must have woken me up. As I lay there, utterly traumatized, I slowly rolled over and opened my eyes. On my wall, inside a large framed picture of Stonehenge, I saw Marial and Monykuoch's faces. They were talking and laughing. It was as though I were watching them on television! I was definitely awake; this was no dream. I rubbed my eyes and looked again, but now all I saw were the rocks in Stonehenge. Feeling sick to my stomach, I decided to skip coffee and go outside for my morning paper. Just outside my door was a black feather shaped like an angel's wings. The sense of knowing it was from Marial overwhelmed me. The spirits of our loved ones seem to know everything we are feeling and thinking and try to send us comfort from the other side. As I finally began to collect myself, I realized that my alarm had not gone off, and I was going to be late for work. I ran into Mom's room to check on her and say that I did not have time to prepare her food. Her only response was, "I saw Marial last night." It was all more than I could wrap my head around. How I was able to focus at work that day I will never know. As bad as that dream was, I have to say the rest was all good.

Two days later, I once again heard birds chirping in the wall. At this point, it no longer startled me. I simply said hello and went about my business. Not only do I strongly believe that the strange happenings or my miracles from heaven (depending upon your viewpoint) have been a major source of my strength but I also perceive them as aiding in my spiritual development. I never was angry at God for taking Marial—quite the contrary. I felt blessed that I had the opportunity to know an angel here on earth, even if it was for only eight short years. The question was becoming very obvious. Why me, why so much activity from the other side? I had queried everyone I knew if they had any unexplainable experiences after a child, parent, sibling, best friend, or spouse had died. Literally everyone had at least one story, but no one had anywhere near as many as I did. I was coming to the realization that maybe it was my destiny to try to open grieving eyes to the immortality of the soul in order to assist in others' healing. It was certainly not in the job description of an exercise physiologist or rehabilitation therapist, and even though I did get a master's degree in counseling many years ago, I do not have a license, so counseling was not an option for me. I needed more than just stories to prove to people what I had come to believe so strongly in my heart about immortality. Marial must have sensed this and figured out a way through photography.

A Celebration and Thanksgiving for Michael Marial Monyjok

Born: August 28, 1984
Born to Eternal Life: August 29, 2009

Saturday, July 17, 2010
Three o'clock in the Afternoon

The Reverend Paul A. Elliott, Th.D.
Celebrant and Preacher

St. Michael & All Angels Episcopal Church
6740 James B. Rivers Drive
Stone Mountain, GA 30087
1-770-469-8551
www.stmichael.cc

Paranormal photography

For months, James had been planning a memorial service to mark the first anniversary of Marial's passing. It was really a logistical nightmare, because the family members were scattered all over the United States and Australia. The timing was tricky because the guys needed to be out of school and to get time off from their jobs to fly to Atlanta. On July 17, 2010, relatives and friends once again gathered at Saint Michael and All Angels Episcopal church to remember Marial This time I was not so strong. I had written pages and pages to eulogize him, but this time I cried through most of it. I took a lot of photographs of the church before I got up to make my speech. I had purchased the camera about three months earlier for around eighty dollars, and it had always taken perfect pictures. I did not look at what I had taken until I got home. What I found was beyond description. It appeared to me that Marial's energy had swooped in every other photo. One would be perfectly clear, and the next, albeit of the same place in the church, was blurs of lights. When I took the guys to the cemetery immediately following the service, the same thing happened, only the ground was also distorted. The pictures appear on the following pages. The ground and land are flat! I have shown these photos to professional photographers, and no one has an explanation. As far as the church goes, I have been back twice, taking the same shots and deliberately trying to move my camera to see if I could replicate the blurriness, and

I cannot! When I returned home, I took more photos. My dining room table was full of framed photos of Marial and his high school diploma. As you will see, the same thing happened at home. It appeared to me that his energy was moving through the room. Look closely until you see the photo with two distinct faces on the wall. Apparently, not only was Marial there, but he brought some family from the other side too!

After I took these pictures, his family and friends arrived for dinner. There were approximately forty people in my house, and I took lots of pictures, and they all came out perfectly normal, that is, until the next morning. David from Chicago and Deng and his wife from Australia spent the night. We were all having breakfast when another relative from Boston came to pick everyone up. I was to take one last picture. When we reviewed it, everyone was pleased, and I promised to e-mail each person a copy. Once they all left, I went back to my camera to review all the pictures. Again I was taken off guard, as the picture of breakfast that we had thought was so good was now terribly distorted. It looked like everyone had two sets of eyes. I knew Marial was in my kitchen. He had been in the dining room, at the church, and at the cemetery. There was no doubt in my mind. Deng had even said to me at breakfast that he'd had the best night's sleep and had "felt Marial's presence." I was so sad when they left, but I had enough cleaning up to do to keep me busy for a few days. I never looked at my camera until two days later. Before leaving for work on an early Tuesday morning, I got the shock of my life. (page 70)

These are the first paranormal photos I have every taken, but they were to become the first of many!

These were taken in the church during our memorial service eleven months after Marial passed. I took a lot of pictures that are in perfect focus, but the following four appear to be distorted by what I am inclined to call *energy*—Marial's energy to be exact. The first was of a table I had set up with three framed photos of Marial on it. Behind the table was a large candelabra with five candles representing Marial and his four deceased siblings. The second photo was of the stained glass window of the Archangel Michael.

I have no idea what the light looks like a check mark is. The large white blob of light under the window is the altar. It is important to note that I have been back to this church several times trying to reproduce these images by shaking the camera while depressing the shutter. I was unable to replicate the effect.

I turned around and faced the back of the church. The photo is of attendees standing and singing. In the back, where there appears to be a bright light, there are large brown doors, which were closed.

Immediately after the service, I took some of his relatives to the cemetery. Earlier in the summer I had planted red begonias in the shape of a cross. Marial's energy began to swoop in over the cross and really distorts the next picture. You can just see the top of the concrete angel at the foot of the grave. Note the large dip in the landscape and wall in the foreground. *This land is perfectly flat*, as you can see in the comparison photo.

When I got home, I took pictures of my dining room table, upon which I had placed white roses, a Black angel, and framed photos of Marial. The first picture has an unusual bright light coming through the glass on the door. Note this is not the sun, as on the other side of that door is another room, which is shaded by trees. The second picture is of the very same door. Look closely below the window. The angel's wing is the left wing but is centered under the window. In the prior shot, the left wing is left of the window. Once again, I have not been able to reproduce the blur of the window with even the most exaggerated movement of the camera. The next two photos will make a believer out of the most diehard skeptic!

This shot was framed exactly as the last one.

I Will Never Leave You

This shot was framed exactly as the last one on the previous page. Note the candle at the very top of the page. It is on a large brass holder. That candle is actually on the other side of the room! Also, note the shift or the angle of the photo. I would have to have been in a mighty contorted position to get that shot!

Rev. Dee Massengale, DD, M.Ed, MA

Two spirit faces, upper left hand corner.

The Light of Love That Is Immortality

I turned my camera on to review the memorial weekend photos with a clear and distinct memory that the last photo I had taken was of breakfast Sunday morning; everyone's faces were distorted. I was not prepared for what I found. There was a bolt of light recognizable as an energy field. I was frozen, astonished, amazed, even numb, until I saw the date at the bottom of the photo. It read 3/28/2009, *my birthday*, but this was July 2010.

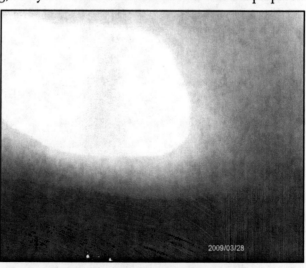

The light of love that is immortality

Now I had received the greatest gift of all: a picture of Marial in spirit. You see, on March 28, 2009, Marial had flown to Atlanta for my birthday. We spent the evening at Medieval Times and had a blast. I even dressed up in period costume and he told me I looked like a princess that night. That princess thing was a running joke, as one of the Lost Boys had given me the name Nanaban, which means princess in Dinka.

This was actually taken on March 28, 2009, the Medieval Times

I honestly felt it was his way of thanking me for having his people over for dinner and for participating in the memorial.

There was a chiropractor who also claimed to be psychic next door to the clinic where I worked. During lunch I beelined it to CVS and got the photos printed. I then took the one of Marial's energy with my birthdate on it to Dr. S Roberts. I handed her the photo and simply asked, "What do you see?"

She responded, "Oh, he is your life guide; he lived longer and accomplished more than ever planned. It takes an angel to attract one." This was only the second time I had walked into her office. The first time was three years before, so she knew nothing of my present circumstances. I did, in fact, have to get and pay for a chiropractic adjustment, as she really does run a chiropractic practice. It was not that

I needed confirmation that Marial was in the photo: I was just curious about what she would say. As you may recall, my place of employment was not exactly open to my newly acquired photography, however, I did put the picture of Marial's energy in the Reiki room with the intention of telling a patient it was just the light that I visualize when working on them, if ever any one was to ask. This photograph still means more to me than a million dollars ever could. There have been so many more pictures *from heaven* I will share with you, but first: a great snake story that reinforces the immortality theme.

Before I started crying during the memorial eulogy, I told three stories, each one depicting a remarkable aspect of Marial's character. In describing his gentle, nonviolent nature I talked about a deadly poisonous snake. The doorbell rang one afternoon. Deb a neighbor, was frantic. "There is a big copperhead snake in my yard; please get Marial to come and kill it." He was busy doing homework but agreed to walk up the street to appease the damsel in distress. She was armed with a large shovel and was shouting at him to chop the snake's head off. Once he received the shovel, Marial fearlessly approached the snake, scooped it up, and tossed it over the fence. Deb was enraged. "Why didn't you kill the damn snake?" she demanded.

His reply was priceless, "That snake never did anything to hurt me." At that, he turned around and calmly walked back home and resumed his studies. Six days after the memorial, I was getting in my car to go to work, and, lo and behold, in my closed garage was a six-foot-long copperhead coiled by the driver's side of my car. I screamed, hit the garage door opener, and screamed some more. I ran out in my driveway and continued to scream, but nobody came. I had to get to work. I thought for a minute and decided to creep back into the garage and enter through the passenger side door. At the time I was still driving Marial's Honda, which would automatically lock the passenger doors when the ignition was cut off. On that day, for some miraculous reason, the door was unlocked, and I was able to get in. I guess by now you know who I believe unlocked the door. The real dilemma came as I pulled out of the garage, staring at this big snake, and knowing I had to make the decision to leave the garage open so it could escape or to close the door so no one could break in. Safety came first, so I hit the door remote and took off. When I got to work I asked every patient what in the world was I to do to get rid of the snake. Without exception, I was advised to chop his head off. Late in the day, Marial's words came back to haunt me: "That snake never did anything to hurt me." By this point, I decided to seek solace from one of the counselors. Jane, who was very open to the paranormal, suggested I Google the symbolism of the snake. What I discovered convinced me that Marial had placed the snake in my garage. According to Wikipedia, a snake represents death and rebirth, immortality, healing, eternity, guardianship, and continual renewal of life. Not only were these profound messages, but I got the feeling that he also appreciated the story I had told at church. My fear of returning home was gone, as in my heart I knew the snake would not be there. My garage door had a small hole where it must have gotten in. I trusted that it made its escape through the same hole while I was at work.

I never saw that snake again.

I told another story during the memorial where I compared the young man I met in 2001 to a little bird who had fallen from the nest and broken his wing. Marial had been wounded in spirit and seemed unsure of his surroundings, but in the following years he metamorphosed into an eagle. A powerful bird, he protected friends, family, and even strangers in every conceivable way. One very rainy night in 2003, Marial and I were on our way to dinner. We came upon a terrible car accident that had just happened. The utility pole was knocked down, and there were wires all over the road. He shouted at me to stop the car, and before I came to a complete stop he had jumped out. Marial wanted to see if the driver was trapped. Not knowing if he even knew what a live wire was, I started screaming for him to stop, but he was a man on a rescue mission and my screams did not deter him. The driver was conscious, and Marial stayed with him until the police and ambulance came. I was still too terrified to go to the accident because of the wires even though I have medical training that could have been helpful. Marial was the hero, the brave one, and at that point the soaking wet one!

On the morning of the memorial, I found a large, black feather lying on my newspaper in the driveway, and on the day after I found the snake in my garage, I received a card with a large eagle on it. I was once again feeling that this was synchronicity, not coincidence, so I Googled the symbolism of the eagle. I discovered that eagles carry our prayers to heaven and are symbolic of immortality, courage, and spiritual protection. The message of *immortality* had certainly presented itself loud and clear over the last eleven months and in so many unique ways. What better gift than to have my deceased loved one find ways to tell me over and over that he is still here?

Orbs

I have taken thousands of pictures in my life. In fact, photography was something of a compulsion of mine for many years, but I never took a single photograph that I would have called paranormal. After taking the memorial pictures, I did not use my camera until I got to the Dominican Republic six weeks later. Once again, there were distortions that I could not explain, but I inherently felt they were proof of Marial's *energy*.

It was two months later that I learned that the largest full moon ever to be seen in my lifetime could be viewed the following night. I invited some friends over for a full moon party and had my camera ready to take pictures. What I got was far more astounding than a large moon. There was an orb in the picture too. Prior to this I had only viewed one photo with an orb in it and that was in my psychic development class. I was ecstatic and my friends were dumbfounded!

I will try to explain what an orb is. In my mind, it is definitely energy. When one zooms in, one can see in great detail fuzzy lines that look like energy. Orbs move, as demonstrated by the picture of my dog Shelby (page 75). They may move in location within a room as seen in sequential photos. For example, you can see in the pictures of me and the twins (page 75) in my living room that first the orb is on my shoulder, and then seconds later it is on the ceiling. Many people, especially psychics, can see faces inside the orb. Most of my pictures

I Will Never Leave You

that have an orb have been the result of my asking, "Are you here?" My feeling is that an orb is an emanation of the spirit and can be detected by a camera when the spirit slows its vibration in such a way that it can be detected as light, i.e. as electromagnetic waves. I feel the spirit chooses to be seen and is trying to let us know that he is all around us. Orbs are highly evolved and can change locations very quickly. Finally, orbs may be the closest thing to proof that energies do exists in another realm, or as I like to put it, that the soul is immortal.

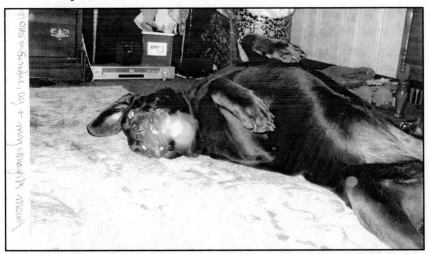

My dog Shelby two months after my other dog Dinkbear died. One orb on her leg, too.

Orb on my shoulder.

It happened two pictures in a row!

It is interesting that my paranormal photography seems to have evolved. It started with what appeared to be blurs created by energy at the memorial. Then I got *the* picture of Marial's *energy*, which I titled "The Light of Love that is Immortality," followed by a combination of orbs and blurred images in Jamaica. I am convinced that Marial was continuing to prove to me that he is still here.

An excellent book on orb photography is *The Orb Project* by Miceal Ledwith, DD, LLD and Klaus Heinemann, PhD. Dr. Ledwith was a professor of theology at Maynooth College in Ireland and subsequently the president of the university. Dr. Heinemann is a physicist and has worked as a research scientist at NASA, UCLA, and Stanford. He has taken over one hundred thousand images of orbs and explains in great scientific detail that they are neither dust nor water particles. It is an intriguing book, albeit a bit over my head.

On my first birthday without Marial, I went to the mountains by myself. As I was preparing to take a picture of the waterfall I asked, "Are you here?"

Ever since the March 28, 2009 photo of the orb or energy, I have continued to see orbs in my pictures in two distinct circumstances. They always appear on special occasions, such as my birthday, Mother's Day, and literally whenever I ask the question, "Are you here?"

My dog, who was very intuitive. September 2010

Night sky. November 2010

I went out on my deck one morning and asked, "Are you here?" June 2011

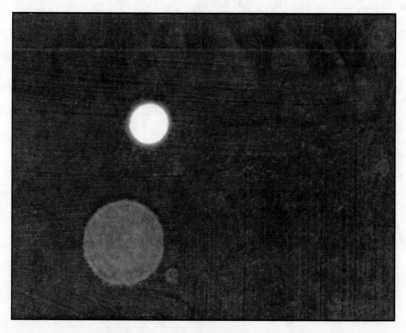

The above orbs was taken at night, when I asked Marial if he were with me.

I Will Never Leave You

I took a few shots into the darkness just outside my bedroom door (on the patio) and got nothing. I then said, "Marial if you are here I want to see you." Most unusual image of energy or spirit. Taken 2/10/2012.

Mother's Day 2011

My mother had only been gone three months. The previous Mother's Day was hard enough, but this year was going to be really tough. I booked a trip to Jamaica to try to escape it. This gift was at Dunn River Falls. As you can see, there is an orb with a dove inside of it. This message was unmistakable. My sweet *bird* wanted to wish me a happy Mother's Day.

On March 28, 2011 I returned to the same park in the mountains where I had spent my last birthday. Once again, I asked, "Are you here?" My whole family showed up!

This is my best friend Zekia. Her birthday happens to be the same day that Marial died. The three of us were to have dinner together on August 31, 2009, but instead she was taking care of me in every way imaginable.

Two years later, I gave her a birthday party. Lots of pictures were taken that night, but this is the only one with an orb in it. I think he was there for her.

The kids set the camera on a table, ran to me and said, "Mike are you here?" Monykuoch is to my left. He is the one who says he talks to Marial in spirit.

Memorial service October 2011 at the Peachtree Christian Church in Atlanta. It was for all members that had passed since last All Saints Day. My cousin Teresa Massengale Rhine and my mother were among those that were remembered that day. There is an orb right by the chandelier.

Celebrating my birthday days later with my best friend Zekia at the St. Regis Hotel in Atlanta.

An orb and two moving energies.

I Will Never Leave You

Walking outside shooting into a dark sky and once again simply saying "Are you here".

Five days after Dinkbear died, I was at a psychic weekend workshop in downtown Atlanta. The blond in the top photo calls herself a pet psychic. I eagerly signed up for a reading, as I was feeling guilty for having to put my dog down even though she was very sick and in a lot of pain. As she began to talk about my dog, she suddenly stopped and said that a tall Black man was standing behind me (in spirit) with his hand on my shoulder. She started to cry as she described the love he felt for me. He told me not to worry, as the dog was with him and he understood I had done what was best for her. After she collected herself, the reading continued with the greatest concentration on my remaining dog Shelby. It was a very different psychic reading, and I took a picture of the psychic in order to better remember it and her technique. When I looked in the viewfinder I found an orb on the table by the psychic's booth. I immediately went back and showed her the orb. Her response was, "I told you he is with you."

This is the most remarkable photograph of all. Look closely and you can see the imprint of a wing. I first noticed it in November 2010 on the window in my meditation room. My first thought was that a bird had flown into the large window and left its impression on the window. A couple of weeks later I was cleaning the window with glass cleaner, and as I rubbed over part of the wing, it went away. The imprint was on the *inside of the window!* Impossible. (I so regret not having taken a photo before I cleaned, but I had no idea what this would come to mean.) Immediately, I felt it was something that Marial had done. I no longer had a camera, so I ran to the pharmacy and bought a ten-dollar throwaway. On the next page, you will see what I got. This particular photograph, however, was taken in January 2012, as the print that I did not erase is still there. I am never going to clean that part of the window!

I tried to take a picture of the wings, but what I got blew my mind. Through the glass and into my backyard, at the top left was a cross and beside it the numbers 1 and 20. This is difficult to see because it was not a digital camera, and there are no negatives, so I can't recreate it. At the bottom of the photo, it looks like a spirit face and up top, it looks like an angel. Deep in the woods, I can see the face of an African man, and it looks like David. I immediately knew that those numbers were a sign, especially since they sat beside a crucifix. What was going to happen on January 20? Was that the day my mom would pass? I initially took the photo to a psychic medium named Susan who verified the numbers and chuckled as Marial came through and admitted to leaving the wing imprint with his fingers. He said, "It is easy for me." She also told me that Marial said he would do it again, but it would be on the glass door in my kitchen. Remember I had been a bit fixated on when

my mom was going to pass, partly out of fear of being alone and partly because I was running out of coping skills. I loved my mom, but her dementia made her a different person, and this was hard on me in so many ways. I contemplated the numbers and determined it meant that Mom would pass on January 20. It turned out that the message was even more profound than that. My mother had a massive stroke on January 15, and I stood shoulder to shoulder with a large cross in my church to eulogize her exactly twenty days later!

The morning the real estate agent came to place the for sale sign on my house, I went out to take one last picture of my front garden and asked Mom if this was ok. When I saw this orb I knew it was her way of saying that it was.

Healing from the other side

When I thought there was nothing else that could shock me, I got an e-mail from Tom in Ohio. Cheryl and Tom had co-instructed my psychic development class with Carl. After the fourth session, they had a falling out with Carl and the couple never returned to Atlanta. It had been almost four months since I had spoken to Tom, who was a retired police officer and now doing Reiki energy healings on a volunteer basis. The e-mail read, "DEE, I have messages for you from the other side. If interested, call me on Saturday morning." Well, Saturday could not come fast enough!

Tom began by telling me that his morning meditation was interrupted each day during the last two weeks by what he referred to as "your friend," who had presented himself as a Black man with blue eyes. Then Tom hesitated. I got that gut feeling what he was about to say was not good, and I was right. He went on by saying, "Be better to your mom, love and forgiveness, love and forgiveness, stop getting upset, forgive and let go; I was only here for a short time but you will soon know why."

I do not know if I was embarrassed or just plain flabbergasted. First I asked him for help, "How do I do this?" At that moment, the book *A Course in Miracles* came off the bookshelf near where Tom was sitting. He calmly informed me that I might want to read that book. How in the world could Tom have known that I was locking myself in my room and having a meltdown every night? I really was at the end of my rope with my mother; it had a lot to do with dealing with the behavioral effects of her dementia and was compounded by my deep-rooted anger. I knew Tom was not in my room, but I was now sure that Marial was, and he did not like what he saw. This was the wake-up call of all wake-up calls. Marial was trying to aid in healing my relationship with my mom, and so he did.

I stopped locking myself in my room and spent more time with my mother. On the days that I worked, I started praying for patience the minute I left the clinic so that no matter what disaster I might find when I got home, I would be able to deal with it in a calm and loving manner. On the four days a week that I was home with Mom, I would do Reiki on her back if it was hurting, and I even offered to take her shopping instead of giving her my usual excuses. Mind you, I had been doing the forgiveness meditation for months and had read the book *Radical Forgiveness*, but to dissolve deep-rooted anger is like pealing a really big onion! In my case, it also took divine intervention.

I would only have six more months with my mom, but they were the best six months that we had shared in over fifteen years. I still thank God, Tom, and Marial for that call, which I am certain changed my life, my mom's soul, and our karma forever. Remember, Marial said he was only in my life for a short time and that I would soon learn why. It was no doubt to heal my most important relationship, the one with my mother. What a blessing, a gift that keeps on giving.

It is now August 2010 and the first anniversary of Marial's passing is fast approaching. He must have felt my sadness and apprehension because his activity picked up quite a bit. After my wake-up call, I started sleeping upstairs in Marial's room because it was right next to my mom and I could hear if she had a nightmare or needed me in any way. On August 2 at 3:00 a.m., I awoke to a very bright light. At first my eyes were closed, but the light was so bright that it woke me up. When I opened my eyes, the room was so bright that all I could see was light. Then it went away. Startled, but not afraid, I lay there for a while but could not go back to sleep. As

I often do, I got up and started my day at 3:20 a.m. I do not know what it was, but I have a strong belief that anything related to or symbolic of light has a quality of godliness and must be good.

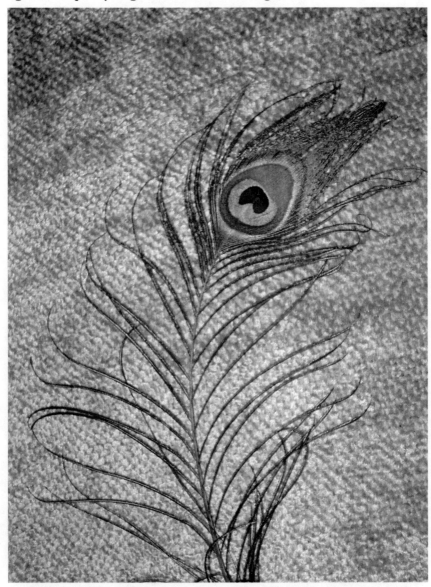

Tom initially took credit for the blue eye bit since he has blue eyes, but so do I. Wrong! Look at a peacock feather and what do you see? It must be that immortality message again!

On August 8, I woke up at 12:12. It was no doubt another sign or warning. Mom's stoke would come in December of that year, and she died in room 12. The next morning I found a plastic angel in my purse just like the one I gave Marial. Impossible; I did not buy it. Was this his way of providing me with comfort after receiving a foreboding message? I definitely connected the dots when I went outside and was nearly run over by a big black butterfly.

A few days later while doing Reiki with a patient at my home, we both heard the birds chirping in the wall for close to five minutes. It was delightful, albeit surreal. For the next two weeks, the bird chirping on my white noise clock would go off by itself almost every other day. Once the button is pushed to start the "rain forest noise," it will stay on unless the electricity goes out. In the summer we have a lot of thunderstorms that do knock out the electricity. This particular clock has to be reset manually, but I have never figured out how to do it. When plugged in, the clock starts at 12:00. If I really want the time to be correct, I have to wait until noon and plug it in. Okay, I am technologically challenged, which is exacerbated by the fact that I hate reading instructions. I am just telling you all of this so you will appreciate the next gift. The clock had been off by hours for days since our last storm. How shocked was I to enter my meditation room and find the clock displaying the exact time? At that point, actually, I was not shocked at all, but I still had to ask the question out loud, "How do you do that?" He should have been an electrical engineer!

On August 23, Mom and I were driving down a long stretch of highway that had one car dealership after another. Without premeditation, I pulled into a Nissan dealer and told the salesman I had to trade the Honda in. It had been a year, and I had to let go of that car and all that it represented. I began to cry as the salesman asked what I was interested in. My answer was bizarre; I just wanted the features that I had in the car that Marial had totaled. I wanted blue tooth capability, leather interior, a sunroof, and interior wood paneling. He took me to a row of Altimas. "I will take the blue one," I told the salesman.

"Okay," he replied and suggested that I take it for a spin. No, I did not want to go around the block; I just wanted to finish the transaction.

At this point, I did not even know how much he would give me for the Honda or how I would pay the rest. Mom was clearly distraught with my demeanor and tears. The salesman came back with the offer; I got out my pendulum and asked Marial if it was okay. It spun counterclockwise, which meant no. I told the man the answer from the spirit was no and that he would have to make me a sweeter deal. This went on for about forty-five minutes. I mainly used the pendulum to freak him out. I was hoping if he thought I was talking to a deceased person about the offer and I was not going to settle until I was told it was a good deal, he might think he was dealing with a demented woman who was not going to back down! It worked; I talked the price down by five thousand dollars and Mom even offered to pay for the car. Maybe they both thought I was crazy. This was way out of character for her, especially since she had developed dementia. She was very worried about spending a dime even though I had tried over and over to tell her that she couldn't take it with her. It was either a final act of love or she knew on some level she wouldn't be needing it. It was a beautiful car, the first brand-new car I have ever owned. One would think that I would have been so happy, but I cried all the way home. Saying good-bye to that Honda was like saying good-bye to Marial all over again.

The next few days were filled with more miracles from the other side. I am reminding you of my interpretation of these events so as to emphasize that each one brought me peace and joy—never, ever any fear. I walked in my meditation room to find the window had come open. I had been told when they were installed how to do this to clean from the other side. It was a manual maneuver, clearly something that the wind could not open. The down side to this was the amount of hot air that had gotten in the room and a client was soon to arrive. A little book titled *Heaven* had been on the window seat and had been knocked to the floor. It is worth noting that the Reiki was really strong that session and I firmly believe I had *help* that day.

The next day I came home after work, turned on the TV to watch the news, and before I knew it the TV switched to DVD. The remote control was on the other side of the room. It was a happy annoyance to have to get up to switch it back. On August 27, I woke up at 4:00 a.m.

to once again find my sheets on the right side of my bed wet, but the bedspread was dry. Thankfully this time I had been sleeping on the left side. The next day I found all the angels knocked over in the mediation room; the glass of the aromatherapy lamp was knocked off; and the side lamp table was unplugged. I swear if I had found this the year before, I would have called an exterminator, convinced that I had rats! I put everything back in its place and never looked for droppings. Instead, I felt blessed by the energy that was being exuded to assure me that I was not going to be alone on the upcoming anniversaries. Tomorrow would be his birthday and the day after, the unspeakable.

On August 28, 2010, I left for the Dominican Republic. Knowing that the anniversary of losing Marial might be tough, I had planned this trip a few months before. As soon as I unpacked, I found a penny in my camera bag that had definitely not been there before. My trip was off to a good start. First stop was a very large and inviting swimming pool. After completing a few laps, I walked to the steps of the pool, and in front of me was the most beautiful black and blond striped feather floating in the water. Wow, just wow, I thought to myself.

Then the sadness started to hit; it was his birthday, but I would not be taking him out for dinner as I had done the last eight years. I cried for a couple of hours but had to pull myself together in the late afternoon. At 4:00, I had booked an excursion to swim with the dolphins. It is something I had always wanted to do, and at this juncture in my life, I thought it would be healing too. I boarded a minivan with two honeymooning couples for the short trip to a touristy marine park. It was one of those places with hidden expenses at every turn. First stop was to have your picture taken being kissed be a sea lion. I wanted the picture, but I did not want to pay twenty bucks for it, so when it was my turn I handed my camera to the guy behind me who agreed to snap the photo of me. When he returned my camera and I looked in the viewfinder, below is what I saw. Impossible! How did this come out of a perfectly clear scene? I had to break down and buy the copy that follows.

I Will Never Leave You

Suddenly, I had that feeling I was being told I was not alone. There were more photos during this trip that are *not of this world!*

The following is what the photograph should have looked like:

This picture was taken while walking down a shady path that led to the ocean and the sea lion show.

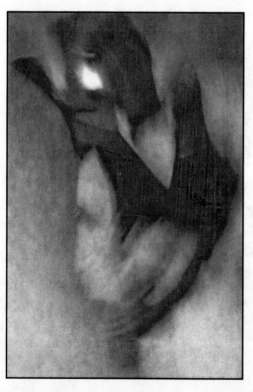

At dinner that night, I asked the waiter to bring me a cupcake with a candle on it. I was going to privately wish Marial a happy birthday. The waiter thought it was my birthday, so all the waiters lined up and started singing happy birthday to me as they approached my table. What you see below is the lead waiter with a bottle of wine followed by the guy with the cupcake. Marial was definitely there; he loved to celebrate his birthday!

The first birthday Marial ever celebrated: August 28, 2002. This is my friend Fred who gave him his first camera that night. My mom was in the hospital recovering from colon cancer surgery.

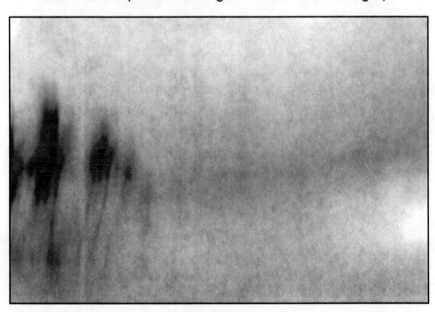

One year to the day to the minute that I was contacted by the detective with the horrific news of Marial's death, I was walking on the beach in the Dominican Republic. All other pictures taken that morning were perfectly clear. It is not even possible to identify the beach, ocean, or coconut trees. I presume his energy is the white seen at the right of the picture. I love this photograph, because I feel he created it to comfort me at a very sad moment. To me, it looks like a Monet.

After returning to my room on that sad morning, I turned on the TV and headed for the shower. As soon as I came out of the bathroom, the TV turned itself off. I was a little startled and said, "Mike?" At that, the TV came back on. A few minutes later, the most amazing feeling of peace came over me while walking to breakfast. A real live peacock crossed my path. It was the only time during the seven days I was in the Dominican Republic that I ever saw a peacock. It was an overwhelming sign that took away my sadness. My only regret is that I did not have my camera with me at that moment.

When I returned from my vacation, I was mortified to discover that the twenty-year-old that I had paid to stay at the house to care for my dogs had thrown a party. I am not going to go into the details of what got broken—it would stress me out too much. The sliding glass doors to my sun room were left open. As I closed them, I literally screamed, "Look at the feathers, they are wings!" My friend Debby was with me and saw it too. We could see wing prints on one of the glass doors. This is very difficult to show accurately, as taking a photo into glass is tricky. The message was very clear, though. Marial had been there protecting my house and had left his signature on the door.

Susan, the medium I had seen six months earlier, told me this was going to happen. I had taken her the photo of the wing imprint from my meditation room to inquire about it. Through channeling, Marial told Susan that he had done it, that it was easy for him and that he would do something again on my kitchen door! Every day for months

I checked the door, looking for a sign. Six months later, when I really needed some peace, it was there.

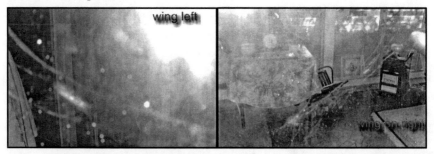

Anniversaries are very difficult, whether it is the first Christmas, birthday, or the actual passing date. They are all a turning point taking us into the next chapter of our lives. This trip was very healing for me, but I know everyone cannot escape to paradise. At the very least, plan ahead to do something gentle for yourself. Get a massage or plan a meal with someone who you know will listen and not be put off if you need to cry. Rituals are helpful, such as lighting a candle by your loved one's picture or writing your loved one a letter and then burning it. Just know that even though it has been a year, it is normal to feel that terrible pain all over again. I cannot emphasize enough that there is no right or wrong way to grieve. Each loss brings different variables that are associated with the relationship and the situation itself. Therefore, every loss will bring its unique grief. Even if what you are feeling is a sense of relief because your loved one is not suffering anymore, it is still a tender time, and you need to be gentle with yourself. No matter what the circumstances of the death, you should expect the unexpected with regard to your emotions and even your reactions to others. No one has a field manual on how to react, or even what to say to someone else in a crisis. If you are grieving and are not hearing what you need, or are hearing what you don't need, it is okay to shield yourself form that friend or family member for a while. If you are the one trying to help a mourning friend and don't know what to say, you got it: say nothing and just listen. At the end of the day, we all just want to be heard and understood anyway. There are far more inappropriate responses than there will ever be words that could somehow miraculously make the whole nightmare go away. On either side of that coin, just do the best you can with what you are given. *I believe* that God does not let someone die to punish us or for any other irrational reason. Death is a part of life, that is a given, and growth does come. Remember the old expression, "that which does not kill me will make me stronger." Well, in many ways it is so true. Through acceptance, we change; through change, we adapt; through adaptation, we grow. If the soul were not faced with challenges, it would never grow, and isn't that why we are here in the first place?

The remaining months of 2009 continued to be filled with miracles from heaven like so many that I have told you: clocks, TVs, and other electronics of all sorts continued to act out. From here on, I will only share extraordinary and unique happenings.

I had taken a medicine wheel workshop with a Canadian Indian in October. We had been instructed to get a picture of ourselves during a very painful time in our lives that we wanted to heal. I chose a picture of me that was taken on my fourth wedding anniversary in Sedona, Arizona. My husband had a way of sabotaging every holiday or special event, and this trip was no exception. I ended up having to hike by myself because he was too hung over. Anyway, we were to wait six weeks then burn the picture and all the negative energy associated with that time would vanish. As fate would have it, I was in Sedona doing a Reiki workshop when my six weeks were up. I was staying in a small bed and breakfast with an outdoor patio. After dinner I decided that patio would be a good place to burn my picture. If you have never been to Sedona, let me tell you it is the blackest sky you will ever see, as there is an ordinance that prohibits streetlights. I lit the match and let the photo burn all the way to my finger, and then I let go. It was so dark that I could not see the floor and just assumed my task was over. The next morning I went out on that patio with my coffee and was dumbfounded at what I saw. There on this pristine clay floor was my face. I tried to scrape it off the floor, but it was like the photo had melted into the patio. I panicked, thinking I was going to have to pay for some ghastly repair to the owner. I went to class and shared my story with the group. One lady suggested that I get nail polish remover to get it up. During lunch, I went to the grocery store bought the polish remover and returned to the bed and breakfast, hoping the proprietor had not seen my face on the patio. For some inexplicable reason when I leaned down to the picture, it moved! It was no longer stuck. It was mine to keep. Not only was it my face, but the remains of the photo were shaped like a heart.

The telepathic message I got was that I was protected and that I would love again. My husband took a lot of my spirit, but he did not take my soul. It was also very clear that my guardian angel or Marial had saved this part of the photograph to remind me that I have survived and will continue to live and thrive with joy. The burnt remains are in a picture frame in my meditation room as a reminder.

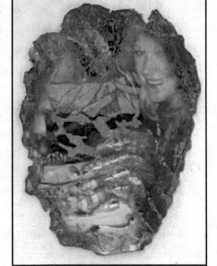

On December 3, I woke up at 3:00 a.m. and went into the meditation room to find water not only all over the floor and carpet, but on the wall too. I have a fountain that water drips down into a bowl. The law of gravity will tell you there is no way that water shot up above this fountain and drenched a photo of me at a waterfall. The most peculiar thing about the picture was that it had water spots all over it in a distorted kind of way. I thought it was a picture that I had printed on my machine and that perhaps the ink was cheap. Compelled to confirm my theory, I went downstairs to get the picture of Marial with the "Mona Lisa look." I knew I had printed that one myself and it was from the same ink cartridge. I went to my chest of drawers where I kept that photo. I pulled out the top drawer on the right, but it was not there. Frustrated, I dumped the contents of that small drawer on my bed, but there was still no picture. Something wasn't right, but I went back upstairs and found that water was once again all over the floor and wall. Mind you, I had already cleaned up once. I was irritated and said, "Mike are you here?" At that moment, my clock starting blinking in seven-second intervals. That went on for about two minutes, and then it resumed normal time. Once again, I cleaned up and felt like I should go look for the picture one more time. I wanted to put it in the water of my fountain and see what would happen. This time I opened the same drawer and there it was just staring at me. The photo is an eight-by-ten, hardly something that I could have missed just minutes before. Relieved, I grabbed the picture and ran upstairs and put the photo under the running water in the fountain, but nothing happened. The ink was not disturbed in any way. I splashed it, but nothing happened. I resorted to immersing his picture in the fountain and left it for an hour. It remained perfectly normal—how could this be? The picture of me was full of spots. To be honest I was overwhelmed, but he was far from finished. I never went back to sleep, but I did return to my room where my white noise machine with ocean sounds was turned off, and I could not get it to come back on. Later on in the afternoon, the white noise machine in the meditation room was also turned off, and the clock read 3:38, but it was actually 4:20. Even though the night before the clock had gone haywire, it had resumed the correct time. Flash forward: I would receive a call from hospice at 3:38 a.m. that my mom had died on February 1, 2011. I turned the bird noise back on, and a few minutes later the clock started flashing for a few seconds. Seven minutes later it flashed again. To actually be in the room with this stuff happening was making me a little nervous. I jerked the plug out of the wall to make it stop. When I plugged it back in, the clock started at 12:00. When I returned ten minutes later, the clock read 1:15. Somebody was obviously trying to make his presence known. This craziness went on in one fashion or another for the next six weeks.

Below is a snapshot of the photo that got ruined by water. Note how far above the fountain, which flows downstream, that my picture is located. Everything about this defies logic.

Rev. Dee Massengale, DD, M.Ed, MA

On the morning of January 15, 2010, my mom got up and approached me in the living room. She looked right at me and called me Ren. That was my father's nickname. He had been dead since 1972 and she never spoke of him; it was just too painful for her. Mom must have seen him standing behind me. Even though she had dementia, she always knew who I was. It was a sign and my heart began to race. Upon the advice of one of the counselors in the clinic, I had been reading *The Tibetan Book of the Living and Dying*. There was a great meditation for the dying where you inhale peace and light and exhale their suffering. I immediately went to my room to do this for my mom.

That very night my mom lay in my lap as we watched our Atlanta Falcons in the Super Bowl. They were playing terribly, and the stress of it was making my back hurt. During half time, I took a hot bath, and when I returned to the TV, Mom looked as if she were asleep. Fifteen minutes into the third quarter, and another interception later, I announced that I was going to bed and suggested she do the same. Mom mumbled no, so I left her on the couch with the TV on. Little did I know she'd had a massive stroke while I was in the bath. Fortunately, our last hours together were soft and tender.

Once in the hospital she came around a bit, but her speech was altered, and she could not swallow or walk. It seemed like a million tests were run only to conclude that it was time for hospice. We were looking at days, maybe weeks. There were two things she said to me during the next fourteen days that meant the world to me. Mom would go in and out of consciousness and every day was different. There was agitation and sedation, attempts to communicate, then nothing. It had been days since she had said anything when out of the blue she said, "Oh, *so beautiful.*"

"What is beautiful?" I asked.

"The *colors,*" she said.

"Mom, do you see the light?"

She responded yes and never said another word that day. I knew she was traveling back and forth, to and from the other side, but this woman was terrified of dying and simply did not want to do it no matter how sick she was. She did not want to leave me either. A couple of days later she said, "Where is the man?"

"What man?" I asked her, and starting naming my male friends. She simply repeated the question. Then I got it. "Are you asking about the man I'm going to marry who I haven't met yet?"

"Yes," she replied. You see, I had been telling her for a year that I was going to get married again and this time he would be kind and I would be happy. I had several psychics tell me this in the past year, and I also felt it in my gut. My mom was so afraid for me to be alone she could not let go until she was reassured there would be someone to take care of me. This demonstrated so much love, a gift indeed.

On the evening of January 31, I left hospice around 10:00 p.m. I was exhausted and my back hurt from lying in the bed with her—the mattress was a joke; it was more sponge than mattress. I knew her time was near. Her breathing was labored; her heart rate was irregular and off the chart; and the mottling in her feet now ran up her legs. I wanted to go home and get a few hours' sleep and then come back. At 3:30 a.m. I woke up, jumped out of bed, and went to the kitchen to make coffee. My plan was to get dressed and go straight to hospice to be with Mom when she took her last breath. No sooner did I take a few sips of coffee than the phone rang. A nurse with an accent said, "Ms. Loyce passed at 3:30." My God, that is the exact time I woke up. First thing I did was go to my meditation room for my journal. It was 3:38, but the clock said 3:30. I could not find my journal, so I went to the computer to send out a mass e-mail, but my energy field was so distressed it took me over an hour to do so. I simply made one mistake after another.

I am ashamed to say that anxiety I felt about not being able to locate my journal, wherein I had documented all my miracles from heaven, was overshadowing the fact I had just lost my mom. I wanted to go back and read the stories of paranormal activity that had gotten me through losing Marial, hoping it would give me some comfort. I literally turned the house upside down: I went through every closet and drawer, and I looked under every piece of furniture. This was particularly surreal because I always kept my journal in my meditation room. I never moved it, but now it was gone and I was sick about it.

When daylight broke, I took the dog out for a brief walk. Halfway home, I looked down and next to the curb was a beautiful purple and white feather. I certainly had never seen a purple bird in the neighborhood. Was this from Mom or was Marial reassuring me I was not alone? I was not sure, but I had a feeling of *just knowing* that it was from one of them. On my drive to hospice to collect Mom's things, a song came on the radio with the lyrics, "I would do anything for you just to make you smile." It is a country and western song that was in an audio card that I had sent to Marial when he was having his troubles in Tulsa. I had the strongest sense he was there trying to comfort me, and so he did.

Once again, I do not remember too much about the next couple of days. Momma's passing came on the heels of losing my godfather in October and my cousin in December. I had to write the eulogy, plan the service, and I wanted to fly Marial's cousin, Aleer, to Atlanta from San Jose to be with me. As far as family goes, Aleer is it. He stepped in as an amazing support system, friend, and brother.

The next few days were full of finding pennies where they should not have been. My angel cards repeatedly read "Hello from Heaven." The miracle of all my little miracles from heaven occurred seven days after my mom died. I opened my sock drawer (as I do every day), and there was my journal just staring me in the face. There is no way on the earth I would have ever put it there, and it had not been there the last six mornings! I was so relieved but somewhat annoyed. Why would he have moved something so important and caused me so much stress?

The message must have been that it was a time to simply reflect on my feelings as they related to my mother. The fact that he did return it was just confirmation that he was there with me to help me along this new journey.

On February 11, I went to see Carl. I wanted to know if Mom would come through and tell me she was happy. He started the reading by saying, "Marial says he borrowed your journal!" You could have blown me over with a feather. Then it got serious as Mom started out by saying she was sorry and that we both learned something. This made me feel sad, but I listened intently as he went on to say what a "classy woman she was in her younger days, very prim and proper. Your dad is with her and he is a very handsome man; she has deep love for him." All of this information was spot on. My mom dressed like a *Vogue* model—prim and proper is an understatement, and my dad was good looking too.

Then Carl told me Mom was showing him a cat. I immediately knew that it must be symbolic because neither my mom nor I ever owned a cat, and, to be honest, we don't even like cats. I just wrote it down and continued to listen. Mom said we switched roles as mother and child, and it was a big lesson for me. The next thing out of Carl's mouth had to come from Mom, because Carl would never have admitted it. He said Mom was pointing her finger at him, telling him, "You disappointed Dee more than once and so have a lot of people." I knew for a fact that Mom was being channeled. Carl had shared with the class something very personal about me that he should not have done and then when I really needed him during my acute grief, he had not returned my e-mail and phone calls. As far as a lot of people disappointing me, that was painfully true. I had not gotten the support from coworkers, neighbors, or cousins that I expected. Even a few close friends did not step up the way I felt they should have. Then Carl told me that Mom was pointing to my throat. He asked if I have spoken up for myself lately.

"Yes, I replied. "In fact, I had confronted little Evie at work. I asked him why he had not passed a condolence to me." When I returned to work, he never told me he was sorry about my mom, but when Marial died, he sent beautiful flowers and came to the wake. Would you believe a licensed counselor's response was, "Well she was old and had been sick." I looked him in the eye and said, "Oh no, you could not be more wrong; her life mattered and you should have honored that with some kind of a verbal hug for me." I'm not sure what else I said, but it was enough to get his blood pressure up, and by the end of the day he was spouting off at me with steam rising from his head. Carl went on to say that little Evie's ego was off the charts and that is why my confronting him had caused so much anger. At the end of the reading, I showed Carl the photo of Mom and me the day before she died. There are mysterious dark shadows all over this picture that I did not understand. When I asked the question,

Marial came through and said, "We were all there: me, your dad, her family—we were all there." Carl then said, Marial is calling it "Reverse black light." Neither Carl nor I were familiar with this terminology but assumed that instead of seeing the spirits in light or orbs, they were in reverse light that was black. The shadows are on top of my head, my arm, below Mom's neck, and especially prominent is the shadow behind her bed. I assure you there was no object there, just a wall.

Mom in bed with dark shadows around her

As soon as I got home I Googled the symbolism of a cat. This turned out to be a powerful message from Mom. According to Wikipedia, the cat reminds us to derive understanding from our internal wisdom. When we turn into our own heart, mind, and soul and trust, we will be shown the truth. It also said that cats are symbolic of reincarnation and psychicism and are synonymous with psychic power. I love this; thanks, Mom!

Once again, spirit communication had given me a great reprieve from grief.

After my mom passed, my grief response was different from what it had been with Marial. He was young and it was a shock; Mom was ninety-two and it was expected. The two weeks in hospice felt like an eternity, but it allowed me to acclimate to the inevitable. I had cried an ocean during her stay there, but I could not cry after she died. For a while I thought something was wrong with me. About a month later, I got a call from the grief counselor from Altus Hospice. She wanted to know how I was doing and if I wanted to come in to talk. It is a free service offered to the family for up to one year. Thinking it might be a good idea, I made the appointment. I spent one hour talking, but frankly I got nothing out of it. This woman was of no help. In fact, all she really said to me was that I was suffering from complicated grief and that I needed to see someone else. She gave me another woman's name and number and that was it. The only reason I decided to see the other counselor was that her office was only minutes from the clinic where I worked. On the afternoon of my appointment I put the address in my GPS, but I failed to find it. I knew I must be driving right by her office, but I could not find it. Frustrated, I picked up my phone to call her, but the battery was dead and I did not have my charger with me. Okay, I refused to give up, so I stopped at a small business and asked if I could use the phone. My call went to the counselor's voice mail. The message started to come through that it was not meant for me to make that appointment, so I went home. What I found upon entering my mom's room was confirmation. Her curtains that had been hanging for years were on the floor. This was clearly spirit activity; curtains do not just fall down. Either Mom or Marial was trying to tell me I did not need counseling. The following photograph was the last piece of the puzzle.

In my psychic development class, we learned a meditation to connect us to our spirit guides. I had identified a Native American chief that I felt compelled to call Chief Howling Wolf. The night the curtains fell, I went into my mediation room and noticed the photo of Marial's energy had condensation under the glass. This was weird because the picture was on a table close to the heat vent and on the other side of the room from the fountain. I did a stupid thing; I put the framed photo on the floor and pressed down on the glass as if to make the condensation go away. Of course the glass broke, but fortunately I did not get cut. I tried to remove the glass but some of it was stuck to the picture because of the moisture. When I pulled the glass off, what was left was an impression of an Indian facing, if not pointing, to the light! Telepathically I heard the message from my guide loud and clear: stay in the light, continue meditating and praying, and everything would be okay. I had just finished reading *Testimony of Light: An* Extraordinary *Message of Life After Death* by Helen Greaves. The author is a nun who channels her friend Sister Frances Banks, formally of the Community of Resurrection, Grahamstown, South Africa. This book had offered me so much inspiration and reinforcement that God is love, love is light, and that God, love, and light are one. Maybe most important, those in the afterlife are in that light of love and God. There could be no coincidence that I had read this book and discovered a metamorphosis of the picture of Marial's energy. Suddenly I remembered a dream I'd had exactly two weeks after Mom died. It was Valentine's Day, and Mom and I always bought each other presents and cards to celebrate. This year the day was uneventful, that is, until I went to sleep. I dreamed that Mom and I were in the living room, and she looked young and beautiful. The doorbell rang and it was the UPS man. He handed me a package addressed to me from Marial Yak. My heart sunk because I knew he was dead. When I opened the box, I found a light bulb like the ones in my dining room crystal chandelier. That is all I remember from the dream. The next morning I recalled my dream so I went into the dining room. When I turned on the light, I found one light bulb had burned out. Maybe it was not a dream but simply a message of light from my loved ones on Valentine's Day. What a gift!

To this day, I continue to put myself in a bubble of white divine light every morning when I meditate and pray. It puts me closer to God and to the other side.

Episodes confirming the paranormal photography continue to exhibit the fact that Marial's determination and unstoppable personality persists on the other side. I had shown a twenty-year-old who claimed to be an aspiring photographer the photos from the memorial service. His opinion was that the shutter speed on the camera had caused the blur. I did not argue because when someone is not open to other possibilities, I do not see that it is my place to try to convince him. His explanation did not consider that my inexpensivecamera did not allow me to alter the shutter speed or to explain why it was that alternate shots of the same frame were in perfect focus, or why the candle from the other side of the room was transposed over the window or why there were faces on my wall. I had to laugh when I got home to find the biggest water mess yet. In my mediation room near the low flowing fountain, there was water all over the hardwood floor; the area rug was soaked; a floor pillow was soaked; and water could even be found on top of the paraffin wax unit, which was a good two feet away from the fountain. There was more water on the ground than the fountain even holds, and it continued to flow. This mess paralleled the chaos I found in my bedroom after the reading from the fraud psychic who had suggested it was my fault that Marial died. In reading back in my journal of this event I had written, "Marial is mad; he has gone over-the-top with water to say to me that the pictures are real." If I had not appreciated his confirmation, I would have been mad too. The hardwood floor had to be re-stained, waxed, and polished; I had to throw away the lavender pillow, and I had to hang the area rug outside for three days. A lot of work!

The following week, I took the picture of his energy to a workshop on psychic investigation. I showed the class and the lecturer my photo. His response was a bit sarcastic, "If you think it is him, so it is." At that very moment the ceiling fan went bonkers; it literally felt like it was going to come out of the ceiling. There was a collective gasp from students, at which time the lecturer said, "Okay, it's him." I really had to smile. The next day I took a picture of my eight-by-ten photo of his energy and on the digital camera's playback, a font appeared that said "detecting a smile." I do not know what that means literally in relation to the camera functions, but I loved that it was the first time it had ever appeared. Remember, I no longer believe in coincidences.

What happened next suggests that my mom and Marial were collaborating to send me a message. First, you should know my mother hated my doves. She insisted they were chickens and if she could have figured out how to open that cage, I very well could have found my birds in the oven. Granted, birds are very messy. Feathers and birdseed is all over the floor five minutes after vacuuming, and there is nonstop poop to clean up, but the chirping is nice. During the warm months, I had the cage out in the sunroom, which is apart from the actual living space in my home. When it got cold, I moved the birds to my mediation room, but that was a problem when I had a client. During a Reiki session when the client was relaxed, the birds would start cooing, which startled and annoyed us both. After Mom died, I put the cage in her bedroom. Bad, bad choice. I should have known she was watching me, and she was furious that those chickens were now sharing her boudoir. Would you believe that the big container of bird food disappeared? Tell me how a huge Tupperware container vanishes from a room. I looked high and low for two days, at which point I drove over to Pet Smart to buy some more food. Upon my return, I plopped down on the love seat that faced Mom's bed and there, by the curtain, was the container of food. I got out my pendulum and once again asked if Marial was behind this prank, and it said yes, but there's no doubt Mom had instructed him to do so. The message was loud and clear that she did not want the chickens in her room, so I moved them once again. I also renamed them—Peace and Forgiveness.

One month to the day after Momma died I had a horrible night. For hours I was choking. I would literally wake up unable to breath. By morning, I was exhausted and felt myself in an acute state of grief. I could not pull myself together, so I called Dr. Smith and told him I was going to be a good hour late to staffing. I had not shed a tear in that clinic since Marial died, and I wasn't going to start now, or so I thought. The minute I arrived, tears welled up in my eyes. The strangest thing is that I did not know what I was feeling so sad about. Five days later I received a phone call from one of Marial's nephews who told me that Marial's mother had died last week. As it turned out, she had died the very day that I was choking, and she had died of respiratory distress! Apparently my energy field was connected to hers too.

A few days later, I stopped Dr. Smith in the hall and told him why I had been late and so upset. He pulled me aside and said, "Dee, I really like you, but please do not let anyone hear you talk that way." He either thought I was crazy or was afraid of the unknown. Either way, I knew it was time for me

Dink Massengale

to get out of there. Never mind that no one in the clinic was on the same page as me with regard to the spirit world; they were also unable or unwilling to lend me any emotional support for all my losses. I was growing more and more weary of my workplace, but I was not in any shape for a big change at that time. I continued to hang in there for a few more months.

On April 8, a freak accident occurred. I was down to one dove as I had given one bird to a friend. Turns out both of mine were male, and as the matured they fought. I had placed the cage out on the deck for cleaning. Shelby, my Labrador bolted out the door after a squirrel and knocked over the cage. Somehow the door came open and my chicken flew away. Understand that a domesticated sub-Saharan African dove does not even have the skill to fly much less find food and survive in the wild. I called my bird day and night for almost seventy-two hours. I could hear him cooing in the trees, but I was unable to lure him back to the deck. I was beyond myself with worry that the bird would surely die if I was unable to retrieve him soon. Finally I went out on the deck on Sunday morning prior to an upcoming thunderstorm and said, "Marial, I know you are out there, so please bring my bird home." I swear that two hours later when I returned to the deck I saw the dove in my neighbor's backyard. I quickly grabbed a paper bag and ran to their yard, where I was able to scoop up my bird and put him in the bag. As I returned him to his cage, I knew that there had been divine intervention in his retrieval. What were the odds I would ever capture a bird?

The day after I recovered my bird, I had a visit from my cousin who lives in Louisiana. It was his sister that had died six weeks before Mom. Since Walter lived so far away, I had been helping clean out my cousin's home and donating her belongings. This was his final trip to Atlanta to settle the estate. He brought along newspaper clippings of our grandfather. He was W. R. Massengale, the founder of the Massengale Advertising Agency that wrote the original ads for Coca-Cola a hundred years ago. He committed suicide shortly after my dad went oversees in World War

II. I was told that he'd had a heart attack. Other than that, Dad never talked about him. I was floored to say the least to discover his nickname was "Dink." Remember Marial was of the Dinka tribe. How do you get the nickname of Dink out of Walter Raymond Massengale? This is not a coincidence, but to be honest it really makes my head spin because I can not imagine what it all means. Could this be a sign that we were all connected? As I was writing this, my computer froze and I had to do a hard shut down and lost the page. At the same time the computer froze, so did my television—I had a picture but no movement or sound. I turned the TV off twice but no change. I believe these are examples of spirit interference. Was it my grandfather?

Pink feet

I know a lot of people think that a medium just tells you what you want to hear. I have always gotten information that no one could make up, but the following is probably the best example of that. About one month before I went in for this reading I had made a new friend who was born and raised in East Africa. She is the daughter of a British diplomat who had recently moved to the States with her husband. I'd had a burning question for a long time and she seemed to be a reliable source. "Jessica, you grew up around Africans. Do they all have pinkish, white skin on the soles of their feet, or did Marial have a pigment problem?" She thought that was the dumbest thing she had ever heard but assured me it was normal. I truly did not dwell on it or give it another minute's thought. When the reading began the first thing out of Susan's mouth was, "The tall man with the big feet is here. He is saying pink feet and is laughing." I almost fell out of my chair. "He says he is happy for you and happy that you are being so generous." I had just left Western Union where I had sent his nephews money and had given his cousin Aleer $700 for his citizenship fee. She said, "He has flowers all around me," and then she asked if this person and I had gone to Jamaica together.

"No, but I am going to Jamaica on Friday."

"He is going with you," she said with a smile. To this day, Susan still says that the pink feet story is one of her favorites.

It was going to be Mother's Day the following Sunday, and I had planned a trip to Jamaica so I would not have to think about the day that Mom and I had always gone out to eat or the day Marial always gave me a sweet card.

The first two nights on the island I got orbs at night in my photographs, but the most amazing is the one featured in the paranormal photography chapter at Dunn River falls. On Mother's Day, I got an orb with a dove in it! I felt as if I had been touched by heaven.

I have had very little spirit communication with or from my mom, but on my first morning in Jamaica I found something that had to have been from her. Mom wore stockings that go just past the ankle. After she died, I gave away all her clothes, even those silly little stockings. Upon arising the first morning, I sat on the edge of my bed and looked down, and there on the floor was one little stocking. I know for a fact I had not packed it; I had not unpacked it; but there it was. I was overwhelmed that she was there with me too!

I had not set an alarm, but at 6:00 a.m. on Mother's Day music came on the radio next to my bed. It was a reggae song with lyrics that go something like this, "you're my angel, my inspiration." That sense of *just knowing* was stronger than I can possibly describe; he was there wishing me a happy Mother's Day.

It was almost the end of May and I was repeating my psychic development class with different students. There was one fascinating young physician that I was paired with to read. He immediately saw a waterfall and a man standing in light. He then told me he saw my backyard and there were black blobs of negative energy, but he said the man in the light was protecting me from it. It was an *oh my God* moment. He then saw a cliff with a tree firmly planted on the edge and said, "You have experienced the edge, but you are firmly grounded now." The next day in class I brought in the photograph of the orb at the waterfall taken on my birthday and he proclaimed, "That is the man I saw in the light." Once again, that feeling of *just knowing* that I was protected and constantly visited from the spirit world gave me pause. For the man who had delivered this message was not only an authentic psychic, he was a medical doctor of psychiatry.

During the last week in May, paranormal activity really picked up. Marial was doing multiple things daily to let me know he was there. It was a sign, unfortunately a sign of yet another tragedy to come. My beloved dog Dinkbear had not been herself since I returned from Jamaica. By May 31, her breathing was labored and she had little energy to walk. I had not taken her to the vet out of pure denial. I loved that dog more than I can express and the thought of anything happening to her was not within my scope of comprehension. She was unable to make it downstairs to my room; instead she had curled up on the floor in Marial's room. I got a blanket and pillow and lay with her, trying to comfort her. By 2:00 a.m., my back really hurt from being on the hard floor, and I moved to the bed. About an hour later I just sat up and I saw Marial standing behind my dog in the doorway of his room. He had his arms crisscrossed over his face, but the rest of him was clear as day. I had a different response than I had from other apparitions of him, maybe because I was already so upset about my dog. I screamed out his name over and over. Eventually, I turned on the light by the bed. At that he disappeared. I immediately knew that Dinkbear was going to die; that is why he had come. The next morning I took her to the vet who found her severely anemic due to an internal bleed. There was nothing that could be done and she was put to sleep. The pain of losing my dog, my friend, felt like the last straw, and my newfound strength was temporarily obliterated.

Two nights later I had the most vivid dream. Dinkbear had escaped from the front door (which she often did) and was running all over my neighborhood. She looked so healthy and happy. I had to believe she was communicating with me the way Mom and Marial had. She was free from her pain and having fun again. I was happy for her but still sad for me. She had been a great dog and I loved her dearly.

On June 11, I got a call from the vet that her ashes were ready for me to pick up. Once again, I found a feather in my car seat. As sad as I was, it really did make me smile. It was like getting a hug when I needed it the most. My little miracles from heaven continued to lift me up.

I have mentioned that I am a bit challenged by technology, the computer in particular, but I do know that the following two incidents will baffle even the brightest computer geek. Just to see if I could figure out how to change my wallpaper or screen saver, I went into my documents folder and clicked on a picture of Marial. I was successful, so I thought I would leave it for a day or so. My laptop is connected to a monitor because I had stepped on it and destroyed the screen. As *you* probably know, when the laptop is shut, the monitor goes to black. The morning that I changed the picture, I closed the laptop and went into the kitchen. About ten minutes later, I heard the noise the computer makes when it is turned on and booting up. It startled me, so I ran into the living room and there was Marial's picture on the monitor, but the laptop was still closed! According to my journal my response was, "Impossible, good morning Mike, and thank you for making me smile."

In early July, Dr. Raymond Moody had invited me to his home in Alabama to experience the psychomanteum. This is a mirror gazing experience that somewhat emulates the ancient Greek gazing at Delphi in hopes of having contact with the deceased. I was told to have one person in mind that I wanted to see. A film team from New York was coming to make a documentary for the A&E Network. The dilemma was in the choice; my dad had been dead for over thirty years, and I would love to talk to him; of course, I wanted to hear from Mom; but knowing what a strong energy Marial is on the other side, I thought the chances of him coming through might be greater. I worried about it all night feeling a hint of guilt no matter what I decided. The next morning I opened up my laptop and found on the screen a picture of Mom and Marial together. It is a really great picture of both of them taken at a restaurant on her ninetieth birthday. This picture said to me not to worry, that they would both come through. I was overcome by a huge sense of relief.

I had read Dr. Moody's book, *Reunions: Visionary Encounters with Departed Loved Ones*. In it, he documents amazing stories of people who have seen three-dimensional apparitions and had conversations with their deceased loved ones in the psychomanteum. Although it does not happen 100 percent of the time, the statistics are good, and I was so excited about this opportunity. It is important for the subject to be relaxed when he goes into the psychomanteum, but this was not the case for me. It had taken all day for the crew to get their lighting just right, and it was some seven hours after I had arrived in Alabama that I actually went into the chamber. I was so tired and really hot. It must have been over eighty degrees in the chamber, and frankly, I was miserable. I had two subtle experiences and one brief apparition. I felt something brush across the side of my face. It was something like a gentle touch and again on my left hand. Was it my mom? I have no way of knowing for sure except for that feeling of *just knowing*. What I did see in the mirror were Marial's legs from the knees down walking gently and slowly through very calm water. This was immediately followed by rushing muddy water in a river. The symbolism so mirrored what was going on in my life. Just the day before, I had quit my job because my workplace had turned into that *muddy river*. I had been through emotional hell there, and walking away from that job without another in place made resigning even more traumatic. I felt the apparition was trying to say that although things felt rough and dark, I needed to stay calm and my situation would have a smooth outcome, and it did. Leaving that negative environment was a very good decision.

The final computer activity happened while being instructed by the twins (age nine at the time) on how to download pictures onto my computer. Out of the blue, a picture of Marial went to my profile picture on Facebook. Did I ever panic! I thought I would die if anyone saw that. People would think I had lost my mind. I began yelling at the kids to delete it, which they did. At first they thought I was mad at them. Monykoush looked at me with wide eyes and said, "I promise I did not do it." Once I calmed down, we were able to laugh about it, and I knew that Marial was there with us.

The Clock

As you may recall, I left my job in July 2011 without another one lined up. Initially I felt the urgency to quickly find employment, but what I did not yet recognize was that I was burned out. The more I looked for work online, the less excited I became about any of the openings I found. Work had never been work for me. I had always followed a passion: my refugee and hospice volunteer work, health and fitness reporting on local TV, and working as a rehabilitation therapist—I loved it all. All of those *jobs* felt like a privilege rather than something I had to do. Once I started writing this book in September, the fire returned and there was no stopping me until I finished. I decided to just put the job thing on the back burner until this manuscript was complete. However, by mid-November I started to worry, and the more I worried, the more chaotic my energy field became. One night I went to bed after stressing over whether I was doing the right thing. Should I make the responsible fiscal decision and just get any job until the right one came along, or should I have faith and continue writing? Somewhere around 1:30 a.m., I woke up to what sounded like very loud ticking. The little bifold clock across the room was ticking so loudly that it woke me up! I had never had an issue with this clock before, but this night was different. I got up and closed the clock, put it on the floor, and muffled it with some pillows. Happily, I was able to go back to sleep. The next morning I made the bed and went across the room to collect the clock. As I opened, it I noticed it was stopped on 12:00. I remember it being past 1:00 when I moved it. Perplexed, I just stared at it, and within approximately thirty seconds, the second hand started to move and the clock was running again. My first thought was that somehow in closing the clock, I'd stopped it, which would still not explain time moving in

I Will Never Leave You

reverse. This was not the case; I opened and closed it several times and the clock never stopped. Once again, I was overcome with that feeling of *just knowing* that it was a sign. Marial was trying to show me the number 12, which I knew meant December or 2012. I was going to get a job in either December or in 2012. The most significant reason I felt like this message was from him was that his picture receiving a literature award is on the right side of the bifold clock. I once again was able to breathe a little easier, as I had received a message that I would get a job when the time was right.

Before I go on, it is worth noting that in December I was offered a job that I had applied for several months before. I rejected it because the salary was not commensurate with my expectations. It was in April 2012 that I decided start my private practice, Good Grief,LLC.

Marial was not done sending me messages through the clocks. It was now January 2012, and I awoke very early and began working on this book. I decided to time myself, just out of curiosity, to see how long it would take me to write one page. I looked at my digital clock at 4:44 a.m. I paid absolutely no attention to the three fours until approximately twenty minutes later. I looked at the clock and it simply read 4. The 4 was in the middle of the screen! It was not in the hour or minutes place. *How weird*, I said to myself, and then it dawned on me—he was trying to send the number four.

I continued to work, glancing at the clock every so often, but the 4 remained in place. Thirty minutes or so passed, and I finally went to my clock and began pushing the off and on buttons. Magically, the correct time appeared. The following three mornings when the alarm went off at 5:00 a.m., my clock read 4, just the number 4! There was no doubt in my mind that a great job was coming in April 2012. Oddly, I had given myself until March 31 to finish the manuscript of this book.

A month later my handy man was at the house replacing a door handle. Out of nowhere he asked, "Are you psychic?"

I laughed and said, "Not really, but some strange things do go on around here." I then took him into Marial's room and picked up the bifold clock. As I began to tell him the story of the clock stopping at 12:00, it happened again! Marial was undoubtedly confirming my story. The clock stopped, not for long, but long enough for the guy to become visibly spooked. He was quite anxious to get out of my house. I guess everyone is not humored by my miracles from heaven.

In all seriousness, I know there are a lot of people who may not buy into anything I have experienced, and that is okay if what I have shared helps or lifts up even one person who is struggling with grief. If you are bereaved, be gentle with yourself and take your time. If you are a friend of the bereaved, be patient and let your friend talk and feel whatever it is at that particular moment. Do not judge. Advice is not necessary but listening is. Check in with your friend on anniversaries, holidays, and special events. Ask if he wants company, but do not push. Just knowing that someone cares and is thinking of you is a tremendous gift.

The goal is to live our lives to the fullest while we are here. To live well we must learn to grieve well. It is a process of healing the heart, soul, mind, and body. To help you along your journey, I would like to recommend the following books.

- *Life After Life,* Raymond Moody, MD
- *Reunions: Visionary Encounters with Departed Loved Ones,* Raymond Moody, MD
- *Healing Words: The Power of Prayer,* Larry Dorsey, MD
- *Testimony of Light: An Extraordinary Message of Life After Death,* Sister Helen Greaves
- *Seeing the Dead Talking to Spirits:* Shamanic Healing through Contact with the Spirit World, Alexandra Leclere
- *On Grief and Grieving,* Elizabeth Kubler-Ross MD and David Kessler
- *Total Forgiveness,* Rev. R. T. Kendall
- *Glimpses of Eternity,* Raymond Moody, MD
- *Letters to a Dying Friend: What Comes Next,* Anton Grosz
- *Your Soul's Plan,* Robert Schwartz
- *I Am Still With You,* Carol J. Obley

- *Memories of the Afterlife*, Michael Newton, PhD
- *Where God Lives*, Melvin Morse, MD
- *Only Love is Real*, Brian Weiss, MD
- *The Tibetan Book of Living and Dying*, Sogyal Rinpoche

Grief

Grief is a lot of things, but most of all it is a process—an unpredictable process. When is it over? That just depends upon how you define it. Acute grief is over when you can think and talk about your loved one without that kick-in-the-gut pain and the urge to cry. If you define grief as the sadness you feel when you think or speak about your loved one, the answer is maybe never. It is normal to feel sad years later because you still miss that person. Time does dull the pain, but if your grief is still acute after two years or so, by all means seek counseling. As painful as so-called normal grief is, it still allows us to return to work, to take proper care of the family that is left behind, and to have aspirations for our future. Maybe the most important aspect is acceptance: without it, moving on is impossible. Dr. Elisabeth Kubler-Ross, renowned psychiatrist in the field of death and dying (the author of sixteen books on the subject) declared five stages of the grieving process.

- **Denial** In the case of a loved one that is terminal, denial occurs when one will not let himself believe the diagnosis. After death, be it anticipated or sudden, denial is that numb state of shock phenomenon that can last for days. It is a result of the pain being more than our psyche can process. If one still does not believe his loved one is dead beyond

the funeral, he should seek help. Obviously denial and acceptance are at polar ends of the spectrum.
- **Anger** These emotions surface when the shock wears off. You may be angry at God, your loved one for leaving you, the doctors, or you may be angry at yourself for "not doing more." Go ahead and scream or break something if you have the urge. Just make sure you feel what you are feeling and do not judge yourself. It is a process!
- **Bargaining** After the anger subsides, the reality of your loss hits. Often people try to bargain with God to relieve their pain. "If I become a better person, will you bring her back? I promise never to yell at her again." Bargaining involves a lot of "what if" and "if only" thoughts, both before and after the death. It is considered to be a tool for the psyche to restore order and to regain its power.
- **Depression** This stage is the empty feeling compounded by the fear that the melancholy will last forever. Grief is a process of healing, and temporary depression is one of the many steps along the way. Depression does need to be medically addressed if you are unable to get out of bed for months, if you stop eating, or have suicidal thoughts. It is appropriate for you to experience your sorrow. It is helpful to tell stories about your loved one. If the listener tells you not to be sad and move on, you should do just that! Move on to a friend or listener who gets it, one who will listen and not judge. Even the best friend cannot properly empathize if he has never walked in similar shoes. I lost quite a few friends because I knew it was better to let them go than have them make insensitive remarks to me.
- **Acceptance** We don't have to understand why someone died; we sure do not have to like it or even be okay with it, but we have to accept as fact that the person is gone. It is the stage where we create a new normal out of a situation that will not even resemble our old normal. Change is difficult,

but it is the seed that takes us to a new level of strength and, hopefully, spirituality.

For much more on the stages, I highly recommend the book *On Grief and Grieving* by Elisabeth Kubler-Ross and David Kessler, published by Scribner 2005.

It is important to note that everyone does not go through all five stages or go through them in the stated order. When the detective drove up to my house, I knew Marial was dead before he opened his mouth. I was definitely in shock but not literal denial. I was able to make multiple phone calls to alert friends and family. Anger took over by the afternoon. One of the very few memories I have of that day was sitting in my living room surrounded by many friends. Out of the blue, I threw my drink at the marble hearth. No one said a word, but the women immediately scrambled to clean up the glass. By the end of the week, my blood pressure had become my biggest concern. My normal 118/70 had soared to 170/110. I think this was a combination of anger, shock, and being in a chronic state of fight-or-flight. I showed up at my primary care doctor without an appointment at noon on Friday and informed the nurse of my blood pressure. When I was told the doctor leaves at noon on Friday and would not see me or write me a prescription, I went ballistic. I had initially explained that I had lost my son and that the wake was in six hours. Did she not care? I started screaming at the nurse and told her that if I have a stroke it would be on their hands. After an hour, the medical assistant came out and took my blood pressure. I was informed if the doctor felt I needed medication she would call it in. One hour later, I got the call that my medicine was ready at Kroger but I was to make an appointment to see the doctor next week. Are you kidding me? Did that witch think I would ever step foot in her office again? It took everything in me not to do something illegal. It is a good thing I did not have a car and that my calm and angelic friend Zekia was driving me around!

The night of the funeral I had a dream that Marial was there on a boat with me. I yelled at him, "What are you doing here? You are dead!" I can remember being so angry at him in that dream. I am pretty sure it was a dream and not a visitation, because he looked a lot older and a bit smug, which was not a personality characteristic of his.

I quickly moved into acceptance as my miracles from heaven began to appear. I completely skipped bargaining and don't believe I ever had real depression. I started to eat after the first week and enthusiastically returned to work the week after the Tulsa trip. Friends invited me over for dinner every weekend and I eagerly went. I often cried, but I did show up. Daily meditation and exercise helped restore my equilibrium. Good nutrition is very important, too, when your body has been through such a shock. Our immune systems are vulnerable, so extra care is important, and don't forget patience. There are no time tables written in stone.

There is no doubt that the paranormal events pushed me along, but so did talking to him. Yes, I would talk to his pictures as if he were actually in the room. It always felt completely natural, but if you are not comfortable doing that, I suggest you write your loved one a letter. You can address any emotion you may be feeling or even talk about unfinished business. Read the letter out loud then go outside and burn it. I did this when Marial's mother died, since I had no way of attending a memorial for her. It gave me closure, and I believe she heard me too.

Now to address the difficult questions you may be contemplating: why has my loved one not shown me a sign, or why have I only seen her once? I can only answer that through my frame of reference. Bear in mind, with as much as *I just know*, there is even more that I do not know.

The only thing I am sure of is that you need to be open and receptive. Start by looking for signs through what I call synchronicity, not coincidence. If this concept is alien to you, I suggest you read *Sign of the Dove* by Mary Rose Occhino. This is an extraordinary book. The author shares her journey of recognizing spiritual signs that had profound effects on her life. Once you start to explore the subject through bibliotherapy, as I like to call it, you will also find that there are no coincidences in the books you are drawn to at any given time. Everything has a reason and a season.

Spirit could be busting its collective backside to let you know he or she is around, but if you are not open, you will not see. With that said, I feel it is also a fact that some souls are more highly evolved than others and making contact is therefore easier. Please understand that does not mean if you only get one sign that your loved one was not a great person or is not showing you love. I think it is a matter of capacity to do so and depends upon where he or she is in his or her soul's journey. From the channelers I have visited in the last two and a half years, I continue to receive the message that Marial is a highly evolved soul. In one reading, he even said that all the stuff he has done in my home comes easily for him. Obviously that is not true for all spirits or everyone would be inundated with activity. Psychiatrist Dr. Raymond Moody says that in his forty years of grief counseling, he has found that the most activity, especially with electronics, occurs after a sudden death. He does not, however, have a theory to explain why. Please take heart and be thankful for the one dream, apparition, or even object that appears out of nowhere as a sign of love on the deceased's part. I know that the deceased are at peace, and they want the same for us. Therefore, the greatest gift we can give our loved one is peace by gracefully moving on.

It is my sincere hope that my stories have opened your eyes and enhanced your hope and faith that the soul is immortal. Most importantly, I hope you realize that love never dies: this ... *I just know.*

Postscript: After I finished this manuscript on March 31, 2012 all paranormal activity stopped for two months. I initially thought that it all had happened so I would write this book for you. Once I licensed my business, Good Grief, LLC, signed a lease, began advertising and designed my bussiness cards the activity started again. It is not very frequent, but often on special occasions or when I am with the twins.

About the Author

Dee Massengale worked as a chronic pain therapist for thirty years. She has her doctorate in divinity with a specialization in grief counseling, is an ordained minister, and also holds master's degrees in both exercise physiology and counseling and psychological services from Georgia State University. Dr. Massengale has a private practice in Atlanta, incorporating a psychomanteum and Reiki into her grief resolution work. In addition, she is a hospice volunteer and has completed her training as a medical assistant in the hope of going to Africa on a medical mission someday.

www.griefresolution.com

CPSIA information can be obtained at www.ICGtesting.com
Printed in the USA
LVOW060012051212

309840LV00003B/154/P